What oth

MW01614912

"Quick and Healthy Meals from Trader Joe's"

"I love the "Quick and Healthy Meals from Trader Joe's" cookbook! My family and I really enjoy trying out the different recipes. Meal planning and shopping are a breeze! It is so easy to put together a delicious healthy dinner. Because of such success, we have even expanded our menus to include foods normally omitted from our diet."

— Sally Kingdon

"I love the recipes! They are really delicious and very easy to prepare. I bought copies for all of my sisters."

— Nadine Hitchcock

"This cookbook has changed the way we eat and has inspired us to eat much more healthfully. My teens are even cooking dinner sometimes now as the recipes are so easy and delicious!"

— Lauren Duensing

"My son who is in college loves this book! He finds the recipes easy and tasty and as he lives near a Trader Joe's, it's also very convenient."

— Jade Luz

"The "Quick and Healthy Meals from Trader Joe's" cookbook is THE BEST!! I just started cooking about 6 months ago and I picked up this cookbook because I adore Trader Joe's and I absolutely love it. The recipes are easy, healthy and, best of all, delicious!! I have friends over for dinner every week and we haven't tried a single recipe yet that we haven't completely enjoyed. Quite honestly, this cookbook has been a huge factor in my weight loss success of the past 6 months. Because I have been able to cook healthier meals at home, I've changed my eating habits resulting in a 51-pound loss over the last 6 months. So THANK YOU!!"

— Emily Callahan

"Jamie's class was great. I have spent many hours and many dollars doing my best to maximize the nutritional value of foods that also happen to be delicious. Now, having taken the class and using the cookbook, I am quickly and easily preparing many new dishes. To my surprise I am also finding significant cost savings!"

— Diane Kern

"I'm a so-so cook and a vegan, so my meals were pretty boring until Jamie showed me how to incorporate sauces, soups and seasonings through her recipes. Now, my meals are tasty and delicious and super-easy to prepare. This is a must-have cookbook for anyone who has a full schedule, wants to eat healthy and wants it to taste good."

— Jamie Vaughn

Other Books by Jamie Davidson

Quick and Healthy Meals using Trader Joe's Products

Simmering Solutions: Healthy Slow-Cooker Recipes

Livin' Lean with Trader Joe's

Quick and Healthy Meals from Trader Joe's®

Jamie Davidson, M.S.

ReSolve Publishing

Walnut Creek, CA

Published by:
ReSolve Publishing
1626 Orchard Lane
Walnut Creek, CA 94595

925-817-8073
Jamie@HealthyTraderJoes.com
www.HealthyTraderJoes.com

To order more copies go to:
www.HealthyTraderJoes.com

Cover design by: Joni Sare
Layout and design by: Joni Sare
www.jonisare.com

ISBN 978-0-9667309-8-2
eBook: ISBN 978-0-9667309-7-5

Disclaimers:
This book is not affiliated with nor sponsored by Trader Joe's Company.

Products featured in this cookbook may only be available in Trader Joe's on the West Coast.

Trader Joe's changes its products often. Inquire at your local Trader Joe's for product availability. Products used in these recipes may or may not be available.

Acknowledgments

I am grateful to Rich, my husband, who has always supported my creative expressions and did so with this project by tasting and evaluating many of the creative expressions included in this cookbook.

Thanks to Joni Sare, who took the designing of this book under her very capable wing and cheerfully and patiently helped to bring it to completion.

I want to thank the hundreds of class participants who have attended my classes and enthusiastically sampled what I had prepared as well as shared their own recipes and ideas.

Finally, I want to thank Trader Joe's for supplying healthy, delicious food products that can be quickly and easily transformed into wonderful meals for those who are gourmet cooks to those who are culinarily challenged and for all of us in between.

Introduction

Trader Joe's began in 1958 as a chain of convenience stores in Los Angeles and has evolved into a unique grocery market with an incredible fan base. Trader Joe's currently has 415 locations in 40 states. They work with a variety of suppliers worldwide and many of their products are made exclusively for them. All Trader Joe's private label products promise to be free of artificial colors, flavors or preservatives; they don't contain MSG or added trans fats. In addition, all of their private label products are sourced from non-GMO (genetically modified) sources. All of their seafood is without sulfites or sodium tripolyphosphate. Frozen chicken is floor raised without hormones. Fresh dairy products do not contain rBST (bovine growth hormone). Information sheets are available upon request at the stores, as well as online, which offer information on specific foods that are fat-free, low sodium, heart healthy, organic, vegetarian, vegan, gluten-free, or Kosher.

I have been teaching a class entitled "Quick and Healthy Meals from Costco and Trader Joe's" in the San Francisco bay area for over 10 years. Hundreds of people have come to learn which healthy products to purchase from Trader Joe's and about how to use those purchases to make delicious healthy meals quickly.

This cookbook is a compilation of many years of accumulated recipes using many of the wonderful products Trader Joe's has to offer. The recipe ideas have come from my own experimentation as well as a variety of sources and have been adapted from recipes from store customers, local Trader Joe's demo employees, assorted online recipe sites and magazines. They have been nutritionally analyzed using information from the product packages as well as from several FDA sources. While they are very good estimates per serving, they may not be exact, depending on many factors.

Trader Joe's products come and go. It is my hope that most of the products featured will be available for you to use for a long time but, if not, I hope you can find a suitable substitute.

What I find exciting about using Trader Joe's products (and teaching others how to use them) is how quick-to-prepare, easy, delicious and healthy meals can be. With many of us having very full lives, knowing how to put together a delicious and healthy meal quickly can make all the difference between eating well and stopping off or going out for perhaps not-so-healthy fast food or take-out.

There are over 90 entrée recipes featured here, and, with the options featured in many of the recipes, there are many many more delicious meals available to you if you care to experiment. Trader Joe's products lend themselves to lots of experimentation.
Have fun creating your own!

Find Weight Watcher PointsPlus® Values online at www.HealthyTraderJoes.com

Jamie Davidson

Contents

Chicken

Mexican

Chicken Salsa Bowl with Mango Pineapple Salsa

Gluten Free

1 pouch (frozen) TJ's Brown Rice
(organic or regular),
or 2 cups cooked rice

1 (15-ounce) can black beans, rinsed
and drained

1 cup TJ's fresh salsa

½ teaspoon cumin, optional

8 ounces TJ's Just Chicken, cut into
small pieces

Lettuce, chopped

Tomato, chopped

½ cup fresh (refrigerated) TJ's Tropical
Mango Pineapple Salsa

Lime wedge, optional

Serves 4

Per serving:
292 calories
0.6 g fat
547 mg sodium
45 g carbohydrate
6.5 g fiber
26 g protein

Option:
Use TJ's Spicy,
Smoky, Peach Salsa
in place of Mango
Pineapple Salsa.

1. Heat rice according to package directions and divide
   between 4 bowls; keep warm.

2. Combine beans, salsa and cumin; heat in microwave for
   2 minutes, or in saucepan for 7 minutes. Keep warm.

3. Warm Just Chicken in microwave for 2 minutes, or in
   saucepan for 5 to 7 minutes.

4. Place bean and salsa mixture over rice.

5. Place chicken on top of bean and salsa mixture.

6. Add chopped lettuce and tomatoes; top with Mango
   Pineapple Salsa and squeeze lime over the top, if desired.

Serve with warmed corn tortillas or baked tortilla chips and
salsa.

Black Bean Soup with
Spicy Jalapeño Chicken Sausage Gluten Free

1 (14.5-ounce) can TJ's Organic
Black Bean Soup

1 TJ's Spicy Jalapeño Chicken
Sausage, chopped

2 tablespoons fat-free sour cream
or nonfat yogurt, optional

Chopped cilantro, optional

Serves 2

Per serving:
150 calories
4 g fat
555 mg sodium
20 g carbohydrate
3.8 g fiber
10 g protein

Options:
Add ½ cup chopped TJ's
(frozen) mango chunks
before heating soup.

1. Combine soup and sausage; heat in microwave for
   3 minutes, or in saucepan for 7 minutes.
2. Top with sour cream and cilantro, optional.

Salsa Verde Chicken Gluten Free

½ cup boiling water

⅓ cup (dry) sun-dried tomatoes, not in oil

2 tablespoons water

½ onion, chopped, or ½ cup TJ's Diced Onions

⅓ teaspoon TJ's Crushed Garlic, or 1 clove garlic, minced

1 (15-ounce) can TJ's Black Beans, rinsed and drained

1 jar TJ's Salsa Verde

1 package TJ's Just Chicken, chopped

2 tablespoons TJ's Balsamic Vinegar

Serves 6

Per serving:
228 calories
1 g fat
677 mg sodium
8.6 g carbohydrate
5.25 g fiber
28 g protein

Option:
To reduce sodium, use a different brand of salsa verde, use no-salt-added black beans, or eliminate sun-dried tomatoes.

1. Pour boiling water over sun-dried tomatoes and set aside.

2. Heat 2 tablespoons water in a skillet over medium-high heat; cook onions and garlic until onion is translucent, about 3 minutes.

3. Drain tomatoes and chop; add to onion and garlic mixture.

4. Add black beans, salsa, chicken and balsamic vinegar; simmer mixture for 5 minutes.

Serve over rice.

Chicken and Salsa Gluten Free

1 package TJ's Just Chicken, cut into bite-size pieces

1 (12-ounce) carton TJ's fresh salsa

1 (15-ounce) can black beans, drained and rinsed

2 pouches (frozen) TJ's Brown Rice (organic or regular),
or 4 cups cooked rice

Chopped cilantro, optional

Serves 6

Per serving:
286 calories
1 g fat
370 mg sodium
34 g carbohydrate
4 g fiber
25.5 g protein

Options:
Mix chicken, salsa, black beans and cilantro together and serve over rice.

Use TJ's bottled Spicy, Smoky, Peach Salsa in place of fresh salsa.

1. Mix ingredients together in a medium saucepan and cook over medium heat about 8 minutes, or microwave in microwave-safe dish about 3 minutes.

2. Top with fresh cilantro, optional.

Serve with salad and corn tortillas or TJ's Brown Rice Tortillas.

Chipotle Chicken Salad

1 cup TJ's Cilantro Salad Dressing, Reduced Fat

Or make your own dressing:

$\frac{1}{3}$ cup chopped fresh cilantro

$\frac{2}{3}$ cup light sour cream, or low-fat plain yogurt, or Greek yogurt

1 tablespoon minced chipotle chile, canned in adobo sauce

1 teaspoon ground cumin

1 teaspoon chili powder

4 teaspoons fresh lime juice

$\frac{1}{4}$ teaspoon salt

Salad:

4 cups shredded romaine lettuce

8 ounces TJ's Just Chicken

1 cup cherry tomatoes, halved

$\frac{1}{2}$ cup diced avocado

$\frac{1}{3}$ cup thinly vertically sliced red onion

1 (15-ounce) can TJ's Black Beans, rinsed and drained

1 (8 $\frac{3}{4}$-ounce) can no-salt-added whole-kernel corn, rinsed and drained, or (frozen) TJ's Fire Roasted Corn, thawed

Serves 4
(serving size is 2$\frac{1}{2}$ cups)

Per serving:
249 calories
8.2 g fat
605 mg sodium
25 g carbohydrate
7 g fiber
23 g protein

Options:
Use kidney, pinto or TJ's Cuban Black Beans in place of black beans.

Use $\frac{1}{4}$ teaspoon powdered cayenne and 3 drops liquid smoke to substitute for chipotle chile if making your own dressing.

Add a spoonful of adobo sauce for a spicier salad.

Adapted from "Cooking Light."

1. If preparing dressing: combine first 7 ingredients, stir well.

2. To prepare salad: combine lettuce and remaining ingredients in a large bowl. Drizzle dressing over salad; toss gently to coat.

Serve immediately.

Chicken and Veggie Tostadas

2 tablespoons water

1 cup chopped red onion

1 cup (frozen) TJ's corn kernels

1 medium zucchini, chopped

12 ounces TJ's Just Chicken, cut into bite-size pieces

1/2 cup TJ's Salsa Verde

1 teaspoon ground cumin

1/4 teaspoon black pepper

3 tablespoons chopped fresh cilantro, divided

Cooking spray

4 (8-inch) TJ's Whole Grain Flour Tortillas

1/2 cup (2 ounces) shredded Monterey Jack cheese

Romaine lettuce, chopped

2 tablespoons lime juice, optional

Serves 4

Per serving:
242 calories
8 g fat
538 mg sodium
25 g carbohydrate
6.5 g fiber
36 g protein

Options:
Replace chicken with ground turkey, tofu, fish, black beans or TJ's Fat Free Spicy Black Bean Dip.

For soft tacos, heat tortilla 35 seconds each in the microwave.

Use reduced-fat Monterey Jack cheese to reduce fat or TJ's Fancy Shredded Lite Mexican Blend.

1. Heat water in a large pan; add onion, corn, and zucchini to pan and cook for about 2 minutes.

2. Stir in chicken, salsa, cumin, pepper and 2 tablespoons cilantro; cook 10 minutes or until liquid almost evaporates, stir often.

3. Preheat broiler; arrange 2 tortillas in a single layer on a baking sheet sprayed with cooking spray. Broil 3 minutes or until lightly browned. Place 3/4 cup chicken-veggie mixture in the center of each tortilla and sprinkle 1/8 cup cheese over chicken. Broil 2 minutes or until cheese melts.

4. Repeat with remaining 2 tortillas.

Top tostadas with remaining cilantro, lettuce and lime juice.

Chicken and Goat Cheese Quesadillas

1 medium onion, sliced into ¼-inch slices

6 ounces (frozen) TJ's Just Grilled Chicken Strips, thawed

1 (4-ounce) can diced chilies, rinsed and drained

4 TJ's Whole Grain Flour Tortillas

3 ounces TJ's crumbled goat cheese (Chevre)

1 tablespoon chopped fresh cilantro

4 teaspoons fat-free sour cream, or fat-free Greek yogurt

Cilantro sprigs, optional

Lime wedges, optional

Serves 4

Per serving:
242 calories
8 g fat
538 mg sodium
25 g carbohydrate
6.5 g fiber
17.5 g protein

1. Brush onion slices with a little peanut or grapeseed oil and grill on hot grill, or on a griddle, about 3 minutes on each side or until onions are brown.

2. Cut chicken into very thin slices.

3. Preheat oven to 400ºF.

4. Place 1 tortilla on a baking sheet coated with cooking spray. Sprinkle 3 tablespoons cheese, half of chicken, onion, chiles and 1½ teaspoons cilantro on tortilla.

5. Top with another tortilla.

6. Make another quesadilla following steps 4 and 5 above.

7. Spray the top tortillas with cooking spray and bake at 400ºF for 15 minutes or until lightly browned.

8. Let cool 5 minutes and cut each quesadilla into 2 halves, making 4 servings.

9. Top each serving with 1 teaspoon sour cream or yogurt.

Garnish with cilantro sprigs and lime wedges, if desired.

Spicy Chicken Chili Gluten Free

4 cups TJ's Free Range Chicken Broth, or TJ's Organic Low Sodium Chicken Broth (both are gluten free)

1½ cups diced onion, or 1½ cups TJ's Diced Onions

1 (4-ounce) can green chilies, drained and rinsed

2 whole medium tomatoes, diced

3 tablespoons TJ's Tomato Paste

2 (15-ounce) cans TJ's Pinto beans, drained and rinsed

1 package TJ's Just Chicken, cut into bite-size pieces

1 to 2 teaspoons cumin

1 tablespoon chili powder

1 teaspoon cayenne pepper, to taste

2 tablespoons cornstarch

4 tablespoons cold water

Serves 6

Per serving:
256 calories
2 g fat
588 mg sodium
17 g carbohydrate
5 g fiber
28 g protein

1. Bring broth to a boil over medium heat; add onions, chilies, diced tomatoes, and tomato paste.
2. Simmer until onions are tender, about 5 minutes.
3. Add beans, cooked chicken and spices to saucepan; simmer 10 minutes.
4. To thicken, add cornstarch to 4 tablespoons cold water and stir; add to chili and stir until chili thickens.

Serve with warm corn tortillas or TJ's Brown Rice Tortillas and salad.

Grilled Chicken Quesadillas

Sauce:

¼ cup TJ's Cilantro Salad Dressing, Reduced Fat

¼ cup TJ's Reduced-Fat Mayonnaise

Freshly ground black pepper

1 chipotle chile in adobo sauce (canned), drained and minced, optional

12 ounces TJ's Just Chicken, or (frozen) TJ's Just Grilled Chicken Strips, thawed, cut into bite-size pieces

½ cup grated TJ's Fancy Lite Mexican Blend Cheese, or reduced-fat Monterey Jack Cheese

8 TJ's corn tortillas

8 tablespoons (refrigerated) TJ's salsa

Serves 4

Per serving:
310 calories
7.8 g fat
342 mg sodium
27 g carbohydrate
3.2 g fiber
34 g protein

Options:
Use ¼ cup light sour cream or yogurt, 1 tablespoon lime juice and 1 tablespoon chopped cilantro if not using TJ's Cilantro Salad Dressing.

Add a tablespoon of TJ's Fat Free Spicy Bean Dip on each tortilla before adding cheese.

1. Heat grill or broiler.

2. For the sauce: in a small bowl, whisk together salad dressing, mayonnaise and pepper. Stir in chipotle chile, optional.

3. Spread 1 tablespoon of sauce on each of the 8 tortillas.

4. Top 4 tortillas each with ¼ of the chicken and 2 tablespoons cheese; cover with remaining tortillas (sauce side down).

5. Grill quesadillas over medium heat in batches uncovered, turning once; heat until cheese melts and both sides are brown, about 2 minutes on each side.

6. Slice each quesadilla into wedges. Top with salsa.

Serve with black beans, rice and vegetables.

Quick Chicken Tortilla Soup

2 tablespoons water

½ onion, chopped,
  or ½ cup TJ's Diced Onions

⅓ teaspoon TJ's Crushed Garlic,
  or 1 clove garlic, chopped

1 cup diced tomatoes
  (fresh or canned)

8 ounces TJ's Just Chicken,
  or 2 cups cooked chicken,
  chopped or shredded

¼ Serrano chili or ½ jalapeno, minced

4 cups TJ's Free Range Chicken
  Broth, or TJ's Organic Low Sodium
  Chicken Broth (both are gluten
  free)

⅛ teaspoon ground cumin

2 ounces TJ's Salted Tortilla Chips
  made with Stone Ground Yellow
  Corn, or reduced fat tortilla chips

2 teaspoons freshly squeezed lime
  juice, or more to taste

2 tablespoons chopped fresh cilantro

Serves 4

Per serving:
157 calories
2.6 g fat
634 mg sodium
14 g carbohydrate
2.8 g fiber
20 g protein

Options:
Top soup with TJ's Fancy
Shredded Light Mexican
Blend cheese.

Top soup with sliced
avocados.

To reduce sodium, use
TJ's Chicken Savory
Broth Reduced Sodium
Liquid Concentrate in
place of TJ's Free Range
Chicken Broth.

1. In a medium saucepan, heat water. Add onions and garlic
   and cook until onions are translucent, about 3 minutes.

2. Add the rest of the ingredients, cover and cook on medium
   heat, stir occasionally for about 15 minutes.

3. Place tortilla chips in each of 4 serving bowls and ladle
   soup over the chips. Add lime juice and fresh cilantro
   and stir.

Cheesy Chicken Enchiladas

8 TJ's Whole Grain Flour Tortillas,
   or whole wheat tortillas

1 (16-ounce) container TJ's Fat Free
   Ricotta Cheese

2 teaspoons TJ's Taco Seasoning Mix,
   or taco or fajita seasoning

1 cup TJ's Fancy Shredded Lite
   Mexican Blend cheese

2 cups TJ's Just Chicken, or (frozen)
   TJ's Just Grilled Chicken Strips,
   thawed, cubed

8 ounces TJ's Enchilada Sauce (bottle)

Serves 8

Per serving:
257 calories
6.3 g fat
457 mg sodium
27 g carbohydrate
6.5 g fiber
22 g protein

Option:
To lower sodium,
use 12 corn tortillas
in place of 8 whole
grain tortillas.

1. Wrap tortillas in a damp paper towel and microwave on high for 60 seconds.

2. Mix ricotta cheese, taco seasoning, ½ cup TJ's Fancy Shredded Mexican Blend cheese and cubed chicken together in a small mixing bowl.

3. Spray an 8 x 8-inch microwaveable dish with vegetable spray.

4. Spread filling evenly on tortillas, roll tightly and place seam side down in baking dish.

5. Pour Enchilada Sauce over tortillas and microwave 10 to 12 minutes until sauce is bubbling.

6. Cover with remaining ½ cup of cheese and microwave for 1 to 2 minutes more.

Chicken

Asian and Indian

Yellow Curry with Chicken and Mushrooms

Gluten Free

2 pouches (frozen) TJ's Brown Rice
   (organic or regular),
   or 4 cups cooked rice

1 package TJ's Just Chicken, diced

1 package TJ's sliced Crimini
   mushrooms (10 ounces)

2 cups TJ's Thai Yellow Curry Sauce

Serves 6

Per serving:
277 calories
5.3 g fat
560 mg sodium
31 g carbohydrate
0.8 g fiber
24 g protein

Options:
Use steamed lentils, shrimp, scallops, tofu, or turkey in place of chicken.

Add ½ cup TJ's Light Coconut Milk.

Add potatoes, parsnips, butternut squash, sweet potato or TJ's Butternut Squash Soup; adjust liquids.

Use other sauces such as Curry Simmer Sauce in place of Thai Yellow Curry Sauce.

1. Heat rice according to package directions; keep warm.

2. Combine chicken, mushrooms and sauce in a microwave-safe bowl and cook 2 or 3 minutes, or until warmed through (or cook in a saucepan for 8 to 10 minutes on medium heat, stir often).

Serve mixture over rice.

Thai Chicken Wraps

½ seedless cucumber, halved
lengthwise and sliced

3 teaspoons chopped fresh cilantro

4 (8-inch) TJ's Whole Grain Flour Tortillas

4 tablespoons TJ's Satay Peanut Sauce

1 package TJ's Just Chicken, cut into
bite-size pieces

Red pepper flakes, optional

Serves 4

Per serving:
303 calories
6 g fat
523 mg sodium
27 g carbohydrate
4 g fiber
35 g protein

Options:
Use shrimp or tofu
in place of chicken.

Use TJ's Thai Yellow
Curry Sauce in place
of satay sauce.

Add fresh chopped
mint.

Use TJ's Brown Rice
Tortillas for a GF version.

1. Combine cucumber and cilantro in a
   bowl; set aside.

2. Heat chicken in microwave for 2
   minutes, or on the stove top for 7
   minutes, or until warmed through.

3. Heat a skillet to medium heat; warm
   each tortilla 15 to 20 seconds on each side. To heat tortillas
   in the microwave: put tortillas on a plate with paper towels
   separating them and cover with a damp paper towel. Microwave for about one minute. To heat in the oven: preheat
   the oven to 250 degrees. Wrap a stack of tortillas in a damp
   dishtowel and place in a casserole dish of similar size. Cover
   with a lid or a piece of aluminum foil tightly on the dish.
   Place in oven for 20 minutes.

4. Spread 1 tablespoon satay sauce on the center of each
   tortilla.

5. Top with ¼ of the chicken and ¼ of the cucumber mixture.

6. Fold the left and the right sides of the tortilla toward the
   center until the edges almost touch. Tightly fold the lower
   2 inches of the tortilla, closest to your body, up over the
   filling. Roll tightly toward the tortilla's upper edge. If the left
   and right sides pull away, tuck them in as you roll.

Thai Curried Chicken

2 tablespoons water

½ onion cut into long slices,
   or ½ cup TJ's Diced Onions

1 cup TJ's Thai Yellow Curry Sauce

½ cup water

2 to 3 small red potatoes, cut into
   16ths

2 medium carrots, chopped,
   or 2 cups TJ's baby carrots

8 ounces TJ's Just Chicken,
   cut into bite-size pieces

½ cup green peas, optional

Chopped fresh cilantro, optional

Serves 4

Per serving:
198 calories
8 g fat
880 mg sodium
14.5 g carbohydrate
2.5 g fiber
15 g protein

Options:
Use sweet potatoes in place of potatoes.

Use tofu, cooked lentils, tilapia or shrimp in place of chicken.

To reduce sodium, reduce Thai Yellow Curry Sauce to ½ to ¾ cup and add water to replace sauce.

1. Heat 2 tablespoons water in a skillet to medium-high heat; add onions and cook until translucent, about 3 minutes.

2. Add 1 cup yellow curry sauce, ½ cup water, potatoes and carrots and cook 15 minutes, or until vegetables are soft when pierced with a fork.

3. Add cooked chicken and peas, if desired, and heat for 3 to 5 minutes, stir often.

Serve curried chicken over rice or serve as a stew.

Top with fresh cilantro, optional.

Curried Chicken Salad with Mango Gluten Free

Chutney Yogurt Dressing:

½ cup low-fat plain yogurt

2 tablespoons Major Grey's Chutney, or TJ's Mango Ginger Chutney

2 teaspoons curry powder, or to taste

⅛ teaspoon ground cumin

¼ teaspoon black pepper, or to taste

Serves 4

Per serving:
160 calories
1 g fat
197 mg sodium
18 g carbohydrate
1.8 g fiber
19 g protein

Salad:

8 ounces TJ's Just Chicken, shredded

1 cup (frozen) TJ's Mango, chopped into ½-inch cubes

1 rib celery, chopped

2 green onions, sliced

1 tablespoon fresh lime juice

Leaf lettuce

Garnish with sliced almond, cilantro, optional

1. Combine dressing ingredients.
2. In a separate bowl, combine salad ingredients and stir together.
3. Pour dressing over the salad and stir gently.
4. Arrange salad on top of lettuce leaves and garnish with almonds and cilantro, if desired.

Chicken Teriyaki Rice Bowls

2 pouches (frozen) TJ's Brown Rice
   (organic or regular),
   or 4 cups cooked rice

1 package (frozen) Trader Ming's
   BBQ Chicken Teriyaki, omit sauce

3 cups broccoli, steamed

1 red bell pepper, chopped

1 can water chestnuts,
   drained and rinsed

¼ cup TJ's Soyaki, or use Soy Vay
   Very Very Teriyaki Sauce

Serves 4

Per serving:
355 calories
5.3 g fat
544 mg sodium
58 g carbohydrate
8.5 g fiber
23 g protein

Option:
Use Trader Joe's (frozen)
Stir Fry Vegetables in
place of vegetables.

1. Prepare rice according to package directions; keep warm.

2. Heat chicken according to package directions; keep warm.

3. Meanwhile, steam broccoli and bell pepper until fork-tender.

4. Add water chestnuts to broccoli and bell pepper; stir well.

5. Divide rice and vegetables between 4 bowls.

6. Place chicken on top of vegetables.

7. Heat sauce and drizzle on chicken.

Serve warm.

Chicken Teriyaki Pasta

6 ounces linguine

2 teaspoons TJ's Grapeseed Oil, or peanut oil

2 carrots, julienne (cut like matchsticks)

1½ cup broccoli flowerettes, cut into bite-size pieces

1 (8-ounce) can sliced water chestnuts, drained

1 (8-ounce) can pineapple chunks or tidbits, drained, or use (frozen) TJ's Pineapple Tidbits

1 package TJ's Just Chicken, cut into bite-size pieces

½ cup TJ's General Tsao Stir Fry Sauce, or other thick teriyaki sauce

Serves 4

Per serving:
441 calories
4.25 g fat
505 mg sodium
63 g carbohydrate
5.8 g fiber
37 g protein

Options:
Add sliced red and/or green bell peppers.

Add red pepper flakes for a spicier version.

1. In a large saucepan, cook linguine according to directions.

2. Add oil to wok or large saucepan and heat to medium-high.

3. Place vegetables, water chestnuts and pineapple in the wok and stir-fry 2 to 3 minutes.

4. Add cooked chicken and teriyaki sauce; stir-fry 3 minutes, just to warm chicken.

5. Drain linguine, toss pasta and chicken mixture together and serve warm.

Apricot Mustard Chicken

1 jar TJ's Organic Apricot Fruit Spread,
  or 10 ounces reduced-sugar apricot jam

1 tablespoon TJ's Dijon mustard

3 tablespoons TJ's Reduced-Sodium
  Soy Sauce

12 ounces TJ's Just Chicken,
  cut into bite-size pieces

1 pouch (frozen) TJ's Organic Brown
  or Jasmine rice, or 2 cups cooked rice

¼ cup TJ's Unsalted Dry Roasted
  Almonds, optional

Serves 4

Per serving:
337 calories
1 g fat
490 mg sodium
52 g carbohydrate
7 g fiber
27 g protein

1. Combine the first 3 ingredients in a bowl and set aside.

2. Heat chicken in a microwave-safe bowl, covered for
   1½ minutes; add sauce and microwave 1 minute more.
   Keep warm.

3. Microwave rice 3 minutes.

4. Serve chicken and sauce over rice.

Serve sprinkled with almonds, optional.

Potsticker Soup

4 cups TJ's Fat Free Chicken Broth

1 cup water

2 packages (frozen) TJ's Stir Fry Vegetables, or 6 cups (total) chopped bok choy and Napa cabbage

²⁄₃ teaspoon TJ's Crushed Garlic, or 2 cloves garlic, minced

2 tablespoons bottled crushed or minced ginger, or freshly grated ginger

½ cup chopped scallions

1 teaspoon TJ's Toasted Sesame Oil

⅛ teaspoon black pepper

1 package (frozen) TJ's Chicken Goyza Potstickers

Serves 6

Per serving:
221 calories
6.8 g fat
731 mg sodium
24 g carbohydrate
2.6 g fiber
13 g protein

Option:
Use TJ's Organic Free Range Chicken Broth-Low Sodium to lower sodium.

Add 2 cups chopped kale.

1. Place chicken broth and water in a 4- to 6-quart pot and bring to a boil.

2. Add frozen vegetable mixture, garlic and ginger. Return to boil, uncovered, stir occasionally for 3 minutes.

3. Add scallions, sesame oil, pepper and potstickers and boil until vegetables are tender and potstickers are heated, about 3 minutes.

4. Divide potstickers among 6 bowls with a slotted spoon; ladle soup over potstickers and serve.

Chicken Vegetable Stir Fry

¼ cup TJ's Fat Free Chicken Broth

3 tablespoons TJ's Reduced Sodium
  Soy Sauce

2 tablespoons dry sherry

1 tablespoon cornstarch

1 tablespoon peanut oil,
  or 1 teaspoon toasted sesame oil
  and 2 teaspoons peanut oil

1 small onion, thinly sliced

⅔ teaspoon TJ's Crushed Garlic,
  or 2 cloves garlic, minced

1 tablespoon bottled crushed or
  minced ginger, or freshly grated
  ginger

4 cups chopped baby bok choy

12 ounces TJ's Just Chicken,
  cut into bite-size pieces

1 pouch (frozen) TJ's Brown Rice
  (organic or regular),
  or 2 cups cooked brown rice

Serves 4

Per serving:
300 calories
3.5 g fat
228 mg sodium
20 g carbohydrate
6.5 g fiber
32 g protein

Options:
If you are not con-
cerned about having
too much sodium in
your diet, you can use
6 ounces TJ's Soyaki
or Soy Vay Very Very
Teriyaki Sauce for first
three ingredients plus
garlic and ginger,
if needed.

Use shrimp or cubed
firm tofu in place of
chicken.

1. Whisk chicken broth, soy sauce, sherry and cornstarch in a
   small bowl until cornstarch dissolves.

2. Heat oil in a large skillet or wok over high heat. Add onion,
   garlic and ginger and cook until onion is translucent, about
   3 minutes.

3. Add bok choy and cook for 2 minutes or until vegetables
   are crisp-tender.

4. Add chicken and heat; add broth mixture and bring to a
   boil, stir constantly.

5. Continue cooking until sauce thickens, about 1 minute.

6. Heat rice according to package directions; keep warm and
   serve chicken over rice.

Teriyaki Chicken, Pineapple and Swiss Cheese Open-Face Sandwiches

2 French rolls (each about 5 inches long and 4 ounces)

1 (12-ounce) package Grilled Teriyaki Chicken Strips

8 canned pineapple rings, rinsed

4 ounces sliced Jarlsburg Lite Swiss cheese

Red onion slices, optional

Romaine lettuce

Serves 4

Per serving:
440 calories
6.2 g fat
474 mg sodium
45 g carbohydrate
3.5 g fiber
39 g protein

1. Horizontally cut each roll in half, and open the rolls to make 4 sandwich bases.
2. Place sliced chicken in a shallow microwave-safe dish and microwave 1½ minutes or until warm.
3. Place chicken, divided evenly, on French bread.
4. Top chicken with 2 pineapple rings; add sliced cheese.
5. Broil in oven until cheese melts, about 2 minutes.

Top with lettuce and onion slices, if desired.

Chicken Wraps with Curry-Mango Mayonnaise

1/2 cup fat-free mayonnaise,
   or fat-free yogurt

1/2 cup finely chopped (frozen) TJ's
   Mango Chunks

3/4 teaspoon curry powder

1/8 teaspoon ground red pepper
   (cayenne)

2 cups TJ's Just Chicken, chopped

1/2 cup chopped red bell pepper

1/4 onion, chopped,
   or 1/4 cup TJ's Diced Onions

4 whole wheat flatbreads

4 red leaf lettuce leaves

Serves 4

Per serving:
382 calories
9 g fat
846 mg sodium
47 g carbohydrate
6 g fiber
31 g protein

Options:
Use (refrigerated) TJ's Mango Pineapple Salsa or Spicy, Smoky, Peach Salsa in place of the mango for extra flavor.

Use whole wheat tortillas in place of flatbreads, or TJ's Brown Rice Tortillas for gluten-free wraps.

1. Combine first 4 ingredients (through ground red pepper) in a medium bowl.

2. Add chicken, bell pepper and onion; stir to combine.

3. Divide chicken mixture evenly among flatbreads (use about 1/2 cup each) spreading to cover half of each flat bread.

4. Top chicken mixture with 1 lettuce leaf. Roll up and serve.

Fruity Curried Chicken Gluten Free

1 cup TJ's Organic Low Sodium Chicken Broth, or TJ's Organic Free Range Chicken Broth

1 onion, finely chopped, or 1 cup TJ's Diced Onions

2 pouches (frozen) TJ's Brown Rice (organic or regular), or 4 cups cooked brown rice

12 ounces TJ's Just Chicken, diced

1 ($8^3/_4$-ounce) can apricots, drained

$1/_2$ teaspoon salt, optional

1 teaspoon curry powder

$1/_4$ teaspoon black pepper

2 tablespoons lemon juice

$1/_3$ cup TJ's raisins

Chopped cilantro, optional

Serves 4

Per serving:
323 calories
2.8 g fat
511 mg sodium
62 g carbohydrate
3.25 g fiber
30 g protein

Options:
If using dried apricots, add 1 tablespoon apricot preserves.

Use 1 cup TJ's Spicy, Smoky, Peach Salsa in place of ingredients apricots through raisins.

1. Heat 2 tablespoons chicken broth in a large skillet on medium-high heat. Add onions and cook until translucent, about 3 minutes.

2. Add the rest of the ingredients and simmer 7 to 10 minutes or until most of the broth has been absorbed.

Garnish with cilantro, optional, and serve.

Spicy Chicken Peanut Soup [Gluten Free]

2 tablespoons water

1 onion, chopped,
   or 1 cup TJ's Diced Onions

1 teaspoon TJ's Crushed Garlic,
   or 3 cloves garlic, minced

1 tablespoon curry powder

1/2 teaspoon black pepper

1 teaspoon red pepper flakes

1 package TJ's Just Chicken,
   cut into bite-size pieces

6 cups TJ's Organic Low Sodium
   Chicken Broth, or TJ's Organic
   Free Range Chicken Broth

1/2 cup TJ's Tomato Paste

1 (15½-ounce) can TJ's Organic
   Tomatoes Diced in Tomato Juice

1/3 cup TJ's Peanut Butter,
   natural style

Chopped cilantro, optional

Serves 8
(serving size is 1½ cups)

Per serving:
172 calories
5.3 g fat
677 mg sodium
9.5 g carbohydrate
2.4 g fiber
22 g protein

Options:
Add 1 cup TJ's Light
Coconut Milk at the end
while heating.

Add 1 red bell pepper,
chopped.

Add chili pepper, crushed
red pepper or Tabasco
sauce for a spicier
version.

1. Heat 2 tablespoons water in large soup pot to
   medium-high heat.

2. Add onions and garlic and cook until onions become
   translucent, about 3 minutes.

3. Add the rest of the ingredients and heat until warm but
   do not boil.

Serve with chopped cilantro, optional.

Szechuan Chicken-Broccoli Slaw Salad

1 package TJ's Organic Broccoli Slaw

8 ounces TJ's Just Chicken, or (frozen) TJ's Just Grilled Chicken Strips, thawed, cut into bite-size pieces

1 ounce chopped roasted peanuts

½ cup TJ's Asian Style Spicy Peanut Vinaigrette

Crushed red pepper flakes, optional

Serves 4

Per serving:
232 calories
3.2 g fat
315 mg sodium
12 g carbohydrate
2.8 g fiber
21 g protein

Option:
Use 2 cups each of shredded Napa cabbage, cabbage and chopped bok choy in place of the Broccoli Slaw.

Add 2 cups chopped kale to salad and add more dressing as needed.

1. Place broccoli slaw in a salad bowl and add chicken and peanuts.
2. Pour dressing and red pepper flakes, if desired, over salad and toss.
3. Season to taste with red pepper flakes, optional.

Thai Chicken Pizza

1 bag (refrigerated) TJ's Wheat Pizza Dough, or prepared pizza crust

7 ounces TJ's Satay Peanut Sauce

4 ounces TJ's Just Chicken, cut into strips

½ cup TJ's part skim mozzarella, shredded

1 bunch green onions, chopped

½ cup fresh bean sprouts

½ cup shredded carrots

1 tablespoon chopped roasted peanuts, optional

Serves 4

Per serving:
380 calories
12 g fat
893 mg sodium
57 g carbohydrate
6 g fiber
21 g protein

Option:
Use prepared pizza crust.

Use 1 cup TJ's Broccoli Slaw instead of bean sprouts and shredded carrots.

Sprinkle chopped cilantro and/or mint over pizza before serving.

1. Place the oven rack on the lowest rung and preheat the oven to 450°F.
2. Form the pizza dough into a circle and place it on a pizza pan sprayed with vegetable oil or olive oil.
3. Spray the surface of the dough with oil and place on the bottom rack of the oven; cook 10 minutes.
4. Spread satay sauce over the partially-cooked pizza crust.
5. Arrange strips of chicken on top. Sprinkle on green onions and cheese.
6. Bake for 8 to 12 minutes on top shelf of oven, until cheese is melted and bubbly. Top with bean sprouts, carrot shreds and peanuts, if using.

Slice into 4 wedges and serve.

Chicken

Everything else

Caesar Chicken Green Salad

1 large head of romaine lettuce, torn

2 cups (8 ounces) chopped
   TJ's Just Chicken

1 cup fat-free or low-fat croutons

1/4 cup freshly grated TJ's
   Parmesan cheese

Dressing:

1/3 cup plain nonfat yogurt, drained,
   or fat-free mayonnaise

2 tablespoons fresh lemon juice

1 teaspoon olive oil

1 teaspoon white wine vinegar

1 teaspoon TJ's Dijon mustard

1 teaspoon anchovy paste, optional

1 teaspoon Worcestershire sauce

1/3 teaspoon TJ's Crushed Garlic,
   or 1 clove garlic, minced

Freshly ground black pepper

Serves 4

Per serving:
188 calories
4.5 g fat
328 mg sodium
11.3 g carbohydrate
2.3 g fiber
26 g protein

Options:
Use bottled fat-free
or low-fat Caesar
dressing.

Use TJ's Low Fat
Parmesan Ranch
Dressing.

1. Arrange torn romaine lettuce in a big serving bowl.

2. Top with chicken and croutons; sprinkle with cheese.

3. Whisk dressing ingredients together and drizzle over salad. Gently toss until combined.

4. Add freshly ground black pepper to taste.

Polenta with Chicken Sausage GlutenFree

2 tablespoons TJ's Organic Low Sodium Chicken Broth

2/3 teaspoon TJ's Crushed Garlic, or 2 cloves garlic, minced

1 (32-ounce) can TJ's Unsalted Whole and Peeled Plum Tomatoes, roughly chopped, with juice

Freshly ground black pepper

1 tube TJ's Organic Polenta

1 cup TJ's Organic Low Sodium Chicken Broth

2 TJ's Spicy Italian Chicken Sausages, cut into 1/2-inch pieces

1 pound TJ's fresh spinach, stemmed, chopped

Serves 4

Per serving:
273 calories
6 g fat
918 mg sodium
34 g carbohydrate
6.7 g fiber
18 g protein

Options:
To reduce sodium, prepare your own polenta with little or no salt.

Use cooked chicken plus other Italian spices in place of sausage.

Add fresh basil.

1. Heat 2 tablespoons of broth in a large saucepan over medium-high heat; add the garlic.

2. Cook 1 minute, stir occasionally; add chopped tomatoes; turn heat to low. Cook sauce until it thickens, about 10 minutes.

3. Meanwhile, slice polenta into large chunks; place polenta and 1/2 cup of the broth in a large skillet over medium heat.

4. Smash and stir the polenta until smooth; add remaining broth. Cook on low until warmed through, about 5 minutes.

5. Add the sausage to the tomato sauce; cook until sausage is heated through, about 5 minutes.

6. Lay spinach on top to steam; cover and cook until spinach is just wilted, 5 minutes. Stir spinach into the sauce.

7. Divide the polenta among 4 bowls; top with sauce.

Blue Cheese-Chicken Salad

Vinaigrette:

2 tablespoons orange juice

2 tablespoons balsamic vinegar

1 tablespoon honey

2 minced shallots

1/4 teaspoon salt

1/4 teaspoon pepper

1 tablespoon olive oil

Serves 4

Per serving:
244 calories
8 g fat
143 mg sodium
23 g carbohydrate
2 g fiber
19 g protein

Option:
Use 6 tablespoons
TJ's Fat Free Balsamic
Vinaigrette Dressing in
place of vinaigrette.

Adapted from "Health."

Salad:

10 ounces TJ's Just Chicken,
  cut into bite-size pieces

1 (10-ounce) package TJ's fresh spinach

1/3 cup crumbled Blue Cheese

1/2 cup TJ's dried sweet cherries

1. Whisk vinaigrette ingredients together and set aside.

2. Place chicken in microwave-safe dish; cover with paper towel and heat for 1 1/2 minutes in microwave.

3. Toss spinach, blue cheese, and cherries in large salad bowl.

4. Whisk vinaigrette and drizzle over salad.

Top salad with chicken and serve.

Chicken Salad Wraps

6 cups chopped romaine lettuce

8 ounces TJ's Just Chicken, chopped

½ cup TJ's bottled Roasted Red Bell
    Peppers, rinsed

¼ cup light Caesar salad dressing,
    or use recipe on Page 47

¼ cup TJ's Roasted Garlic Hummus Dip

4 TJ's Whole Grain Flour Tortillas,
    or TJ's Whole Wheat Lavash Bread

Serves 4

Per serving:
294 calories
8.5 g fat
324 mg sodium
32 g carbohydrate
7.6 g fiber
27 g protein

Option:
Use TJ's Low Fat
Parmesan Ranch
Dressing in place
of light Caesar.

*Adapted from
"Cooking Light"
magazine.*

1. Combine first 4 ingredients.

2. Spread 2 tablespoons hummus over each wrap.

3. Top each wrap with about 2 cups lettuce mixture and roll up.

4. Cut each wrap in half crosswise and serve.

Chicken Alfredo

4 ounces fettuccine

1 teaspoon olive oil

²/₃ teaspoon TJ's Crushed Garlic, or 2 cloves garlic, minced

2 cups sliced mushrooms

2 cups (8 ounces) TJ's Just Chicken, chopped or shredded

1 cup fat-free or low-fat cottage cheese or ricotta cheese

¼ cup skim milk (more if you want it thinner)

¼ cup (½ ounce) freshly grated Parmesan cheese

¼ teaspoon freshly ground black pepper

Serves 4

Per serving:
217 calories
4.2 g fat
396 mg sodium
25 g carbohydrate
2 g fiber
29 g protein

Options:
Add 10 ounces chopped cooked spinach after cheeses have melted.

Add 3 diced Roma tomatoes.

Add 2 cups chopped broccoli and 1 cup diced zucchini and ½ cup chopped red bell pepper.

Add 1 teaspoon dried Italian seasoning when adding mushrooms and other ingredients.

1. Cook pasta according to package directions, drain and keep warm.
2. Heat oil in skillet or saucepan on medium-high heat. Add garlic and sauté about 2 minutes.
3. Add mushrooms, chicken then other ingredients. Turn heat to low, stir constantly until cheeses are melted.
4. Serve over fettuccine or over steamed asparagus or other vegetables.

Butternut Lentil Stew with Chicken

1 small sweet potato, peeled and cut
  into one-inch cubes

2 small red potatoes, cut into fourths

2 tablespoons water

1 onion, chopped,
  or 1 cup TJ's Diced Onions

1½ cups TJ's Curry Simmer Sauce

4 ounces TJ's Just Chicken, chopped,
  or cooked chicken breast

1 cup TJ's Butternut Squash Soup

2 cups refrigerated TJ's Steamed
  Lentils

1 teaspoon curry powder

Serves 4

Per serving:
340 calories
3.6 g fat
711 mg sodium
52 g carbohydrate
11.6 g fiber
22 g protein

Option:
Use TJ's Low Sodium
Butternut Squash Soup
to reduce sodium.

Add mango chunks
just before serving.

1. Place sweet potato pieces and red potato quarters on a microwavable plate and microwave for 2 to 3 minutes or until the pieces can be easily punctured with a fork. Set aside.

2. In a skillet, heat water over medium-high heat and add onions; cook until translucent, about 3 minutes.

4. Add the rest of the ingredients and heat through.

Serve with salad and gluten-free bread.

Bulgarian Turkey Wraps

2 tablespoons water

1 onion, chopped,
or 1 cup TJ's Diced Onions

1 teaspoon TJ's Crushed Garlic,
or 3 cloves garlic, minced

8 ounces TJ's Ground Turkey Breast

1 red bell pepper, chopped

2 medium tomatoes, chopped

½ cup TJ's Eggplant Garlic Spread

4 tablespoons chopped parsley

2 cups sliced TJ's Crimini Mushrooms,
or 2 cups sliced mushrooms

4 TJ's Whole Grain Flour Tortillas

2 cups fresh spinach

4 tablespoons (refrigerated) TJ's
Tahini Sauce

Serves 4

Per serving:
362 calories
10 g fat
556 mg sodium
40 carbohydrate
8 g fiber
24 g protein

Options:
Use yogurt in place of tahini.

To lower carbohydrates and/or sodium, wrap turkey mixture in lettuce.

Use pita bread, naan or flatbread in place of tortillas.

1. In a large skillet, heat water and cook onion and garlic over medium-high heat until translucent, about 3 minutes.

2. Add turkey and cook thoroughly; stir constantly until turkey is brown, about 7 to 9 minutes.

3. Add bell pepper, tomato; cover and simmer for 5 to 6 minutes, stir occasionally.

4. Add eggplant garlic spread, mushrooms and parsley and cook for another 2 minutes, stir occasionally.

5. Heat a skillet to medium heat; warm each tortilla 15 to 20 seconds on each side.

6. Spread the tahini in the middle of the heated tortilla and place the turkey mixture over it. Add the spinach and wrap the burrito, see heating and wrapping instructions, page 30.

Honey Mustard-Peach Salsa Chicken GlutenFree

$2/3$ teaspoon TJ's Crushed Garlic,
or 2 garlic cloves, minced

2 tablespoons light Honey
Mustard dressing (Newman's and
Ken's are gluten free)

2 tablespoons rum, brandy,
or whiskey, optional

1 package TJ's Just Chicken,
cut into bite-size pieces

1 onion, sliced,
or 1 cup TJ's Diced Onions

1 red bell pepper, sliced

1 green bell pepper, sliced

2 large carrots, thinly sliced

Vegetable or olive oil spray

$3/4$ jar TJ's Spicy, Smoky, Peach Salsa

Serves 6

Per serving:
160 calories
1.6 g fat
237 mg sodium
19 g carbohydrate
1.5 g fiber
24 g protein

Options:
Make your own Honey
Mustard dressing
by combining the
following:

$1/2$ cup low-fat plain
yogurt

$1 1/2$ tablespoons light
mayonnaise

2 teaspoons honey

$2 1/2$ teaspoons Dijon
mustard

$1 1/2$ tablespoons fresh
lemon juice

1 scallion, minced

1. Combine garlic, Honey Mustard
   dressing, and optional liquor in a
   shallow large bowl. Add chicken,
   immersing in dressing; set aside.

2. Preheat oven to 375ºF; arrange onions, peppers, and
   carrots on a large baking dish sprayed with oil. Bake for
   20 minutes, turning after 10 minutes.

3. Place vegetables in a microwave-safe baking pan; layer
   chicken over vegetables and spoon salsa over chicken,
   using about $3/4$ of jar.

4. Microwave until the chicken is warm, about 3 minutes.

Serve with rice, quinoa or other grains.

Fried Rice Italiano with Chicken Sausage Gluten Free

2 TJ's Sun Dried Tomato Chicken
   Sausages

1 teaspoon olive oil

½ teaspoon TJ's Crushed Garlic,
   or 1 clove garlic, minced

2 pouches (frozen) TJ's Brown Rice
   (organic or regular),
   or 4 cups cooked rice

1 jar TJ's Bruschetta,
   or 1 container fresh bruschetta

3 tablespoons capers

1 tablespoon dry red wine,
   optional

TJ's fresh Parmesan Cheese,
   optional

Serves 4

Per serving:
258 calories
8.75 g fat
745 mg sodium
48 g carbohydrate
6 g fiber
14 g protein

Options:
Use TJ's Spicy Italian
Chicken Sausage in place
of the Sun Dried Tomato
Chicken sausage.

Add fresh chopped basil.

1. Dice sausage into small pieces.

2. Heat olive oil in medium saucepan on medium-high heat; add garlic, rice and sausage; sauté for about 3 minutes.

3. Add Bruschetta, capers and wine; stir until warm.

Enjoy with a sprinkle of Parmesan cheese, if desired.

Chicken Caesar Penne Pasta

6 ounces penne pasta

12 ounces TJ's Just Chicken, sliced

4 cups thinly sliced romaine lettuce

1½ cups halved cherry tomatoes

½ cup thinly sliced fresh basil

½ cup chopped green onions

½ cup fat-free Caesar salad dressing or make your own (see recipe on page 47)

¼ cup chopped fresh parsley

4 ounces TJ's Light Feta Cheese, crumbled

⅓ teaspoon TJ's Crushed Garlic, or 1 clove garlic, minced

Serves 4

Per serving:
(with Kraft Fat Free Caesar Italian Dressing)
338 calories
8.2 g fat
773 mg sodium
36 g carbohydrate
3.6 g fiber
37 g protein

Options:
Use whole wheat penne pasta to increase fiber.

Use TJ's Cilantro Salad Dressing in place of Caesar.

1. Cook pasta according to package directions; cool to room temperature.
2. Combine all ingredients in a large bowl; toss well to coat.

Chicken Sausage Pizza

1 bag (refrigerated) TJ's Wheat Pizza Dough

Olive or vegetable oil spray

1 cup pizza sauce, spaghetti sauce or marinara sauce

1 TJ's Sun-Dried Tomato with Basil and Tomatoes Chicken Sausage

Fresh basil, tomatoes, artichoke hearts, optional

½ cup part-skim mozzarella cheese

Serves 4

Per serving:
382 calories
11 g fat
741 mg sodium
53 g carbohydrate
7.5 g fiber
18 g protein

Options:
Use other flavors of chicken sausage in place of Sun Dried Tomato with Basil.

1. Place the oven rack on the lowest rung and preheat the oven to 450°F.

2. Form the pizza dough into a circle and place it on a pizza pan sprayed with vegetable oil or olive oil.

3. Spray the surface of the dough with oil and place on the bottom rack of the oven; cook 10 minutes.

4. Spread the tomato sauce evenly over the partially-baked crust to within ½ inch of the edge.

5. Place sausage and optional items over the sauce and sprinkle cheese over the pizza.

6. Place the pizza on the top shelf of the oven and bake for 10 to 15 minutes or until crust is brown.

Chicken BBQ Pizza

1 bag (refrigerated) TJ's Wheat Pizza Dough, or prepared pizza crust

Olive or vegetable oil cooking spray

2 tablespoons TJ's Fat Free Chicken Broth

¾ cup bell pepper strips or (frozen) TJ's Mélange-à-Trois

¼ cup chopped red onion

¼ cup TJ's BBQ sauce

4 ounces (frozen) TJ's Just Grilled Chicken Strips, or cooked chicken breast, sliced into thin strips

Serves 4

Per serving:
319 calories
4 g fat
839 mg sodium
53 g carbohydrate
7 g fiber
10 g protein

1. Place the oven rack on the lowest rung and preheat the oven to 450°F.

2. Form the pizza dough into a circle and place it on a pizza pan sprayed with vegetable oil or olive oil.

3. Spray the surface of the dough with oil and place on the bottom rack of the oven; cook 10 minutes.

4. Add chicken broth to a skillet and heat to medium-high heat. Place bell peppers and red onion into the skillet and cook until peppers are limp, about 3 minutes.

5. Spread BBQ sauce evenly over partially-baked pizza crust.

6. Place chicken and pepper/onion mixture on pizza and place on top shelf of the oven. Cook for 10 to 15 minutes or until crust is brown.

Chicken Cheese Pizza

1 bag (refrigerated) TJ's Wheat Pizza Dough

Olive or vegetable oil cooking spray

3 ounces TJ's Crumbled Goat Cheese (Chevre)

1/2 cup TJ's Fat Free Ricotta Cheese

4 ounces (frozen) TJ's Just Chicken Grilled Chicken Strips, thawed, thinly sliced

1 cup halved TJ's canned artichoke hearts, rinsed and drained

2 large plum tomatoes, diced

2 tablespoons grated Parmesan Cheese

1 tablespoon chopped fresh oregano

Serves 4

Per serving:
389 calories
11 g fat
806 mg sodium
53 g carbohydrate
8.7 g fiber
24 g protein

Options:
Use 1/2 cup TJ's Bruschetta in place of tomatoes, dropping 1/2 teaspoon of bruschetta randomly over cheese base.

Omit chicken for vegetarian version.

Use prepared pizza crust.

1. Place the oven rack on the lowest rung and preheat the oven to 450°F.

2. Form the pizza dough into a circle and place it on a pizza pan sprayed with vegetable oil or olive oil.

3. Spray the surface of the dough with oil and place on the bottom rack of the oven; cook 10 minutes.

4. Mix goat cheese and ricotta in a bowl; spread evenly over partially-baked pizza crust, leaving a 1-inch border.

5. Top with chicken, artichokes and tomatoes; sprinkle with Parmesan.

6. Place pizza on the top shelf of the oven and bake about 10 to 15 minutes or until crust is brown.

Sprinkle with fresh oregano and serve.

Seafood

Mexican

Baja Fish Tacos Gluten Free

Nonstick cooking spray

¾ pound Mahi Mahi, or other firm white fish fillets (thawed if frozen)

2 teaspoons TJ's Taco Seasoning Mix, or taco or fajita seasoning

2 cups sliced green cabbage (about 6 ounces)

1 tablespoon fresh lime juice

½ teaspoon salt

4 tablespoons chopped fresh cilantro

8 TJ's corn tortillas or Brown Rice Tortillas

2½ tablespoons reduced-fat sour cream, divided, or nonfat Greek yogurt, optional

½ avocado, pitted and diced, optional

Fresh or bottled salsa

Lime wedges

Serves 4
(serving size is 2 tacos)

Per serving:
235 calories
6 g fat
507 mg sodium
28 g carbohydrate
6 g fiber
20 g protein

Options:
Use TJ's Cilantro Salad Dressing thickened with a little reduced-fat mayonnaise or low-fat yogurt in place of sour cream.

Adapted from "Health" magazine.

1. Lightly spray grill rack with cooking spray; preheat grill.

2. Sprinkle both sides of fish with taco seasoning, gently pressing into flesh. Grill fish 3 to 4 minutes on each side or until fish flakes easily when tested with a fork.

3. Flake fish into pieces with a fork; keep warm.

4. In a small bowl, mix together cabbage, lime juice, salt and cilantro.

5. Wrap the tortillas in paper towels and microwave 20 seconds on HIGH or until they're warm.

6. Spread fish and cabbage mixture on each tortilla; top with 1 teaspoon of sour cream and avocado, if desired.

Serve with salsa and lime wedges on the side.

Shrimp Tacos with Mango Salsa

2 tablespoons water

1 medium onion, cut into ¼-inch slices

1 pound (frozen) TJ's cooked medium shrimp, tails off, rinsed and drained

½ teaspoon freshly ground black pepper

2 tablespoons fresh lime juice

4 tablespoons chopped fresh cilantro, optional

8 TJ's corn tortillas, or TJ's Brown Rice Tortillas

¼ cup fat-free sour cream or fat-free Greek yogurt

8 tablespoons (refrigerated) TJ's Mango Pineapple Salsa

Serves 4

Per serving:
246 calories
5.7 g fat
480* mg sodium
29 g carbohydrate
3.7 g fiber
27 g protein

*Assuming that rinsing shrimp will decrease sodium by one-third.

Options:
Use 2 tablespoons TJ's Cilantro Salad Dressing mixed with 2 tablespoons reduced-fat or fat-free mayonnaise in place of sour cream.

Use scallops, tilapia, tuna or other firm fish in place of shrimp.

Use TJ's Spicy, Smoky, Peach Salsa in place of Mango Pineapple Salsa.

1. Heat water in a large skillet over medium heat; add sliced onion, cook until translucent, about 3 minutes.

2. Add shrimp and heat for 4 minutes or until warm.

3. Remove from heat and add black pepper, lime juice and cilantro, if desired.

4. Cover each tortilla with damp paper towel and microwave for 20 seconds.

5. Spread shrimp mixture on each tortilla; top with sour cream and salsa.

Chili Scallops with Black Bean Salsa Gluten Free

1 tablespoon chili powder

1 teaspoon sugar

1 pound (frozen) TJ's Scallops

2 teaspoons TJ's Grapeseed Oil
or peanut oil

1½ cups TJ's bottled or fresh salsa

1 (15-ounce) can TJ's Black Beans,
rinsed and drained

2 to 3 tablespoons chopped fresh
cilantro

Serves 4

Per serving:
245 calories
3.6 g fat
667 mg sodium
25 g carbohydrate
4.5 g fiber
25 g protein

Options:
Use TJ's Cuban Black
Beans in place of
Black Beans.

Add frozen corn.

1. Mix chili powder and sugar together; add scallops,
   tossing to coat.
2. In skillet, heat oil until hot; add scallops and cook
   3 to 6 minutes, until scallops are opaque.
3. Combine salsa with black beans and place over scallops.

Serve with rice and garnish with cilantro.

Fish or Shrimp with Cilantro Sauce Gluten Free

16 ounces rock cod, shrimp, or other white fish (thawed if frozen)

1 teaspoon TJ's 21 Seasoning Salute

4 tablespoons water

1 onion, thinly sliced

1 cup TJ's Black Beans, drained and rinsed

2 cups shredded cabbage

1/2 cup (refrigerated) TJ's Cilantro Salad Dressing Reduced Fat

1 pouch (frozen) TJ's Brown Rice (organic or regular), or 2 cups cooked rice

4 tablespoons chopped fresh cilantro

Serves 4

Per serving:

293 calories

4.8 g fat

354 mg sodium

33 g carbohydrate

9 g fiber

27 g protein

Option:

Use TJ's Cuban Black Beans in place of black beans.

1. Wash fish and pat dry. Sprinkle seasoning on both sides of fish or shrimp and press lightly into fish.

2. In a large skillet, heat water. Add onions and cook until translucent, about 3 minutes. Add fish or shrimp, cover saucepan and cook until fish flakes easily with a fork, about 5 to 7 minutes.

3. Add black beans and shredded cabbage and stir. Cover and steam about 3 minutes. Add Cilantro Salad Dressing and stir.

4. Heat rice according to package directions; keep warm.

5. Place fish or shrimp over rice. Top with chopped cilantro.

Tilapia with Peach Salsa Gluten Free

2 tablespoons water

1 onion, chopped,
   or 1 cup TJ's Diced Onions

24 ounces tilapia (thawed if frozen)

1 cup TJ's Spicy, Smoky, Peach Salsa

Nonfat yogurt, optional

Serves 4

Per serving:
194 calories
3 g fat
179 mg sodium
6.25 g carbohydrate
1 g fiber
34 g protein

Options:
Use ahi tuna, salmon, shrimp or chicken in place of tilapia.

For a real change in direction, use TJ's Curry Simmer Sauce, Thai Yellow Curry Sauce, Corn Salsa, or Bruschetta in place of the peach salsa.

1. Cook onion in water heated in skillet until translucent, about 3 minutes.

2. Add tilapia and cook until it flakes with a fork, about 7 minutes.

3. Divide tilapia and onions between 4 plates and top evenly with peach salsa.

4. Add yogurt, optional.

Serve with rice and vegetables.

Seafood

Asian and Indian

Stir Fry Vegetables with Shrimp

2 tablespoons water

1/3 teaspoon TJ's Crushed Garlic,
  or 1 clove garlic, minced

1 package (frozen) TJ's Stir Fry
  Vegetables

12 ounces (frozen) TJ's Medium
  Cooked Shrimp, thawed and rinsed

1 pouch (frozen) TJ's Brown Rice
  (organic or regular),
  or 2 cups cooked rice

2 tablespoons TJ's General Tsao Sauce

2 tablespoons Hoisin sauce
  (available at Asian grocery as well
  as other grocers)

1/8 teaspoon red curry paste, optional

1/4 cup chopped cilantro, optional

Serves 4

Per serving:

300 calories
2.8 g fat
670 mg sodium
43 g carbohydrate
4.75 g fiber
25 g protein

Options:
Add two more
tablespoons General
Tsao Sauce to replace
Hoisin Sauce. Replace
General Tsao and
Hoisin sauces with TJ's
Satay Peanut Sauce or
TJ's Asian Style Peanut
Vinaigrette.

1. Heat large skillet over medium heat; add water and cook garlic for about 2 minutes.

2. Add vegetables and stir often for 2 minutes.

3. Add shrimp, rice and sauces. Stir while heating for about 2 more minutes.

4. Stir in curry paste and cilantro (optional) and serve.

Ahi Tuna in Curry Simmer Sauce Gluten Free with Mango Salsa

14 ounces (frozen) TJ's Ahi Tuna,
cut into 1½-inch cubes

½ cup TJ's Curry Simmer Sauce

¼ cup water, or more

10 ounces (frozen) TJ's spinach,
or fresh spinach

Mango salsa:

1 cup (frozen) TJ's Mango,
cut into ½-inch squares

¼ cup finely chopped red onion

¼ cup chopped cilantro

¼ cup lime juice

2 to 3 drops red pepper sauce

2 teaspoons TJ's Rice Vinegar

Pinch of red pepper flakes, optional

Serves 4

Per serving:
180 calories
2.7 g fat
426 mg sodium
20 g carbohydrate
3.3 g fiber
24 g protein

Options:
Use TJ's Spicy, Smoky,
Peach Salsa or TJ's
Tropical Mango Pine-
apple Salsa in place of
mango salsa.

Use tilapia, chicken,
shrimp, scallops or tofu
in place of ahi tuna.

1. Place tuna, curry simmer sauce and water in a medium saucepan; cook on medium heat for 5 to 6 minutes, stir often. Fish will be cooked when all sides are opaque.

2. Microwave or steam spinach according to package directions; keep warm.

3. Mix salsa ingredients together and stir. (May be prepared up to a day before and refrigerated.)

4. Divide spinach between four plates. Place ¼ of fish on top of spinach and top with mango salsa.

Serve with rice or quinoa.

Curried Lentil-Spinach Salad with Shrimp

Gluten Free

Mint dressing:

1/4 cup chopped fresh mint

1/4 cup fresh lemon juice
   (about 2 lemons)

2 tablespoons honey

2 tablespoons TJ's Dijon mustard

1 tablespoon extra-virgin olive oil

1 tablespoon water

1 1/2 teaspoons curry powder

Serves 4

Per serving:
283 calories
4.75 g fat
557 mg sodium
36 g carbohydrate
10.5 g fiber
23 g protein

*Adapted from
"Cooking Light."*

Salad:

8 cups TJ's fresh spinach, torn

2 cups TJ's sliced mushrooms

1 red bell pepper, cut into 1/4-inch strips

2 cups (refrigerated) TJ's Steamed Lentils

1/2 pound (frozen) TJ's cooked medium shrimp,
   thawed and rinsed

1. Combine mint with the next 6 ingredients; set aside.
2. Combine 1/4 cup of mint dressing, torn spinach, mushrooms, and bell pepper; toss well to coat.
3. Combine lentils and 1/2 cup mint dressing; toss well.
4. Arrange 2 cups spinach mixture on each of 4 plates; top each serving with 1/2 cup lentil mixture.
5. Divide shrimp among salads; drizzle with remaining dressing.

Lemon-Basil Shrimp with Rice Gluten Free

½ teaspoon hot chili flakes

1½ teaspoons shredded lemon peel

2 tablespoons lemon juice

3 cups TJ's Organic Low Sodium Chicken Broth, or TJ's Organic Free Range Chicken Broth

1 pound (38 to 50/lb) frozen cooked, or uncooked deveined TJ's Shrimp

4 tablespoons cornstarch mixed with 3 tablespoons water

2 tablespoons chopped fresh basil leaves

Water chestnuts, sliced red bell peppers, optional

1½ pouches (frozen) TJ's Brown Rice (organic or regular), or 3 cups cooked rice

Serves 4

Per serving:
326 calories
2.3 g fat
228 mg sodium
41 g carbohydrate
1.6 g fiber
32 g protein

Option:
Add ½ cup light coconut milk after adding basil; warm mixture. Do not boil.

Add sliced bell peppers, snow peas, bok choy or other vegetables.

1. In a 12-inch frying pan or a 5- to 6-quart pan over high heat, combine chili flakes, lemon peel, lemon juice and broth.

2. When mixture boils, add shrimp and stir often. If using raw shrimp, cook until shrimp are opaque but moist-looking in the thickest part.

3. Stir cornstarch mixture into pan; stir until mixture boils again.

4. Add basil and other vegetables, if desired.

5. Heat rice according to package directions and mound it equally into wide bowls; ladle shrimp mixture around rice mounds.

Seared Curry Salmon

½ cup TJ's Curry Simmer Sauce

4 (4-ounce) salmon fillets with skin

Dressing:

3 tablespoons TJ's Rice Vinegar

5 teaspoons TJ's Reduced Sodium
  Soy Sauce

1½ teaspoons TJ's Toasted Sesame Oil

1 tablespoon chopped fresh cilantro

¾ teaspoon minced ginger

½ teaspoon sugar

2 pouches (frozen) TJ's Brown Rice (organic or regular),
  or 4 cups cooked rice

1 package (frozen) TJ's Stir Fry Vegetables

Serves 4

Per serving:
451 calories
14 g fat
842 mg sodium
32 g carbohydrate
5 g fiber
42 g protein

1. For salmon: Place salmon fillets, skin side down, on baking sheet. Spread curry simmer sauce over salmon; cover with plastic and refrigerate at least 30 minutes.

2. For dressing: whisk ingredients in small bowl; set aside.

3. Spray vegetable oil in skillet over medium-high heat. Add salmon fillets, flesh side down, to skillet. Sear until brown, about 3 minutes. Turn fillets over and sear skin side until salmon is just cooked through, about 3 minutes.

4. Prepare rice and vegetables according to package directions, omit oil, using water or broth instead.

5. Spoon rice onto plates, dividing equally. Top each serving with seared salmon fillet, then vegetables. Drizzle dressing on salad.

Serve extra dressing separately.

Shrimp Mango Stir Fry Gluten Free

2 tablespoons water

½ onion, chopped,
  or ½ cup TJ's Diced Onions

1 package (frozen) TJ's Mélange-à-trois
  (frozen bell pepper mixture)

½ package (frozen) TJ's Mango Chunks

1 package (frozen) TJ's cooked medium
  shrimp, thawed

2 pouches (frozen) TJ's Rice (Brown or
  Jasmine), or 4 cups cooked rice

Serves 4

Per serving:
344 calories
1.5 g fat
292 mg sodium
56 g carbohydrate
7.5 g fiber
24 g protein

Option:
Use 1½ cups TJ's
Spicy, Smoky,
Peach Salsa in
place of Mango
Chunks.

1. Heat 2 tablespoons water in a wok or skillet over medium-high heat and cook onion 3 minutes; add peppers and cook until crisp-tender.

2. Add mangos and stir until thoroughly heated.

3. Add shrimp and heat until shrimp is warm.

4. Heat rice according to package directions.

Serve shrimp mixture over rice.

Biryani with Shrimp

1 tablespoon TJ's Organic Low Sodium Chicken Broth, or TJ's Organic Free Range Chicken Broth

½ onion, chopped, or ½ cup TJ's Diced Onions

1 package (frozen) TJ's Vegetable Biryani with Vegetable Dumplings

36 TJ's medium-size cooked shrimp, tail off

1 teaspoon ground turmeric

¼ cup raisins

Serves 3

Per serving:
248 calories
6 g fat
682 mg sodium
42 g carbohydrate
3.5 g fiber
17 g protein

Options:
Add (frozen) TJ's Stir Fry Vegetables, cook until warmed through.

Use cooked chicken, scallops, TJ's Steamed Lentils, lean beef strips or tofu in place of shrimp.

Add TJ's Mango Chunks.

Add TJ's Curry Simmer Sauce and/or TJ's Light Coconut Milk.

Add TJ's Thai Yellow Simmer Sauce.

1. Heat broth in a saucepan over medium-high heat.

2. Add onions and cook until translucent, about 3 minutes.

3. Reduce heat to medium; add Biryani and dumplings, shrimp and turmeric.

Stir and heat for 5 minutes, or until warmed thoroughly.

Halibut in Thai Curry Sauce over Polenta

1 tube TJ's Organic Polenta

1 teaspoon red curry paste, or to taste

10 ounces TJ's Light Coconut Milk

1/4 cup fresh basil, chopped

2 tablespoons TJ's Reduced Sodium Soy Sauce

2 tablespoons brown sugar

2/3 cup TJ's Fat Free Chicken Broth or vegetable broth

2 tablespoons fresh lime juice

2 medium zucchini, chopped

2 tablespoons corn kernels

2 medium red bell peppers, chopped

8 to 10 ounces TJ's Crimini mushrooms, sliced

1 pound halibut, skinned and cut into 4 pieces

Serves 4

Per serving:
324 calories
6.8 g fat
796 mg sodium
34 g carbohydrate
4.3 g fiber
29 g protein

Options:
Use perch, salmon, snapper or grouper in place of halibut.

Use TJ's Low Sodium Chicken Broth to lower sodium.

1. Mash polenta and place in microwavable dish; cover with a paper towel and set aside.

2. Combine curry paste with coconut milk in a large heavy skillet and simmer on medium-low heat for 5 minutes.

3. Add basil, soy sauce, sugar, broth, lime juice, zucchini, corn, peppers and mushrooms; simmer for 4 more minutes.

4 Add halibut and simmer, covered, for 10 minutes or until halibut is opaque and cooked through, turning once.

5. Set aside and keep warm.

6. Microwave polenta 2 minutes and divide it onto 4 plates.

Serve halibut over polenta with curry sauce ladled on top.

Seafood

Everything else

Smoked Salmon Salad GlutenFree

3 cups salad greens

1 cup fresh or frozen corn, thawed

4 ounces TJ's sliced smoked salmon

1 tablespoon toasted pine nuts

1 ounce TJ's Crumbled Chevre (goat cheese)

1 tablespoon finely chopped fresh dill or 1 teaspoon dried dill weed

2 tablespoons (refrigerated) TJ's Champagne Pear Vinaigrette

Freshly ground black pepper, optional

Serves 2

Per serving:
163 calories
10 g fat
672 mg sodium
12 g carbohydrate
2 g fiber
15 g protein

Option:
Use TJ's Low Fat Parmesan Ranch in place of dressing.

1. Divide the greens and corn between two plates. Set aside.

2. Cut the salmon into thin strips and scatter strips over each salad.

3. Top each salad with half the pine nuts, goat cheese and fresh dill.

4. Drizzle dressing over salads and sprinkle with pepper, if desired.

Salmon Pasta Salad

8 ounces TJ's Fusilli, cooked al dente and drained

1 (7½-ounce) can TJ's Pink Salmon, rinsed and drained, or fresh cooked Salmon

1 (10-ounce) can TJ's Artichoke Hearts, rinsed and drained

1 cup (frozen) TJ's peas, thawed

½ green bell pepper, thinly sliced

½ red bell pepper, thinly sliced

3 whole green onions, thinly sliced

1 teaspoon vegetable seasoning

¼ cup chopped fresh dill, or 2 tablespoons dry and 2 tablespoons fresh chopped parsley

½ cup low-calorie Italian salad dressing mixed with 2 teaspoons TJ's Dijon mustard

Serves 6

Per serving:
261 calories
9 g fat
411 mg sodium
36 g carbohydrate
3.7 g fiber
16 g protein

Options:
Use TJ's Balsamic Vinaigrette or TJ's Fat Free Balsamic Vinaigrette in place of low-calorie Italian dressing.

Use whole wheat fusilli to increase fiber.

Adapted from "Deliciously Simple."

1. Place all ingredients with the exception of dressing in large bowl. Toss gently until combined.

2. Sprinkle with salad dressing and mix gently.

3. Chill 20 to 30 minutes before serving.

Savory Scallops

1 tablespoon butter or margarine

1 pound (frozen) TJ's Scallops, thawed (10/20 size), cut in half, if desired

½ cup dry white wine, or reduced-sodium chicken broth

1 container or jar of TJ's Bruschetta

8 ounces TJ's whole wheat pasta, cooked as directed

Grated Parmesan cheese, optional

Serves 4

Per serving:
422 calories
9.2 g fat
698 mg sodium
63 g carbohydrate
6.5 fiber
30 g protein

Option:
Use white fish, shrimp, seafood medley or tofu in place of scallops.

1. Melt butter in a large skillet.

2. Add scallops and sauté for 3 minutes on medium-high heat.

3. Add wine or broth and sauté 3 more minutes until liquid is slightly reduced.

4. Add bruschetta and stir until warm, about 2 to 3 minutes.

5. Serve over hot pasta.

Sprinkle with Parmesan, optional.

Veggie Shrimp Gumbo Gluten Free

1 bag (frozen) Trader Joe's Shrimp Stir Fry

1 can (14.5 ounce) TJ's Organic Tomatoes
   Diced and Fire Roasted

1 pouch (frozen) TJ's Brown Rice,
   (organic or regular)
   or 2 cups cooked rice

Serves 4

Per serving:
151 calories
1 g fat
560 mg sodium
30 g carbohydrate
3 g fiber
8 g protein

Option:
If you can't find
fire-roasted
tomatoes use
1 can diced
tomatoes and
add a drop or two
of liquid smoke
to the tomatoes
before adding to
the dish.

1. Prepare the stir-fry according to package directions, using
   water in place of oil.

2. Add tomatoes and cook until heated through.

3. Microwave rice 3 minutes and add to shrimp mixture
   and stir.

Tuna and White Beans Italiano Salad Gluten Free

1 (5-ounce) can TJ's Solid White Albacore, packed in water, drained and rinsed

1 (15-ounce) can TJ's Cannellini Beans, rinsed and drained

2 tablespoons red wine vinegar

½ cup TJ's Bruschetta, fresh or bottled

¼ cup chopped red onion

¼ cup fresh basil

Romaine leaves

Serves 4

Per serving:
160 calories
2 g fat
351 mg sodium
19 g carbohydrate
6 g fiber
17 g protein

Options:
Use fresh tuna.

Add capers, red bell pepper and/or sliced Kalamata olives.

Add artichoke hearts or any of TJ's tapenades.

Use TJ's Balsamic Vinaigrette Salad Dressing in place of red wine vinegar.

Mix ingredients; place on romaine and serve.

Balsamic-Glazed Halibut `Gluten Free`

2 tablespoons balsamic vinegar

1 teaspoon firmly packed brown sugar

1 teaspoon TJ's Dijon mustard

2 pieces halibut (each about 1-inch thick and 5 to 6 ounces)

½ teaspoon olive oil

Salt and pepper, optional

Serves 2

Per serving:
210 calories
5 g fat
154 mg sodium
2.7 g carbohydrate
0 g fiber
35 g protein

Adapted from "Sunset."

1. In a bowl, mix vinegar, brown sugar, and mustard.
2. Rinse halibut and pat dry. Brush lightly with oil and sprinkle with salt and pepper, if desired.
3. Heat a large skillet over medium-high heat.
4. Add fish and cook until browned on the bottom, about 4 minutes.
5. Turn pieces over. Spoon vinegar mixture over browned sides. Lower heat and cook until fish is opaque but still moist-looking in the center (cut to test); cook 4 to 5 minutes longer.
6. Transfer to plates.

Serve with rice and vegetables.

Seafood Pasta Marinara

8 ounces TJ's spaghetti

2 tablespoons water

1 teaspoon TJ's Crushed Garlic,
  or 3 cloves garlic, minced

$\frac{1}{2}$ onion, chopped,
  or $\frac{1}{2}$ cup TJ's Diced Onions

$\frac{1}{2}$ teaspoon red pepper flakes

1 package (frozen) TJ's Seafood Blend

$\frac{1}{4}$ cup Sauvignon Blanc

1 (28-ounce) can TJ's Tuscano
  Marinara

Black pepper, to taste

Fresh basil, cut into thin strips

Freshly grated Parmesan cheese,
  optional

Serves 6

Per serving:
285 calories
2.4 g fat
658 mg sodium
41 g carbohydrate
5 g fiber
20 g protein

Option:
Use whole wheat
spaghetti to increase
fiber.

Note:
Use shrimp, scallops
and/or cracked crab in
place of Seafood Blend.

1. Prepare spaghetti according to package directions.

2. In large skillet, cook garlic and onions in 2 tablespoons water, about 3 minutes.

3. Add pepper flakes and seafood; pour in wine and simmer until liquid is reduced by half, about 10 minutes.

4. Add marinara sauce and season with pepper. Bring to a boil; add cooked pasta; toss to mix. Garnish with basil and serve.

Sprinkle Parmesan cheese over the sauce, if desired.

Scallops Dijon

8 ounces TJ's linguine

2 tablespoons water

¾ pound (frozen) TJ's Scallops, thawed and rinsed

½ teaspoon extra virgin olive oil

1 medium red bell pepper, chopped (about 1 cup)

1 cup chopped red onion

½ teaspoon TJ's Crushed Garlic, or 1½ cloves garlic, minced

⅔ cup white wine

3 tablespoons TJ's Dijon mustard

¼ cup chopped parsley

Serves 4

Per serving:
352 calories
2 g fat
413 mg sodium
50 g carbohydrate
3 g fiber
21 g protein

Options:
Use whole wheat linguine to increase fiber.

Use (frozen) TJ's Seafood Blend in place of scallops.

1. Prepare linguine according to package directions; keep warm.
2. While linguine is cooking, heat 2 tablespoons water in a skillet; add scallops and cook 3 to 6 minutes, or until opaque.
3. Heat olive oil in a skillet over medium-high heat.
4. Add bell pepper, onion, and garlic, sauté until vegetables are soft.
5. Add scallops; cook another minute.
6. Add wine; simmer 2 minutes.
7. Stir in mustard and add parsley; heat through.

Serve over linguine.

Shrimp Italiano

8 ounces TJ's linguini,
   or use fresh linguine

2 teaspoons low-sodium chicken
   broth

1 pound (frozen) TJ's cooked
   medium shrimp, thawed and
   rinsed

1 cup TJ's Roasted Garlic Spaghetti
   Sauce

Freshly grated Parmesan Cheese

Serves 4

Per serving:
360 calories
3.5 g fat
400 mg sodium
43 g carbohydrate
5.5 g fiber
35 g protein

Options:
Use scallops, chicken or
cubed tofu in place of
shrimp.

Use whole wheat linguini
to increase fiber.

1. Cook linguine according to package directions; keep warm.

2. Heat broth in skillet over medium-high heat until hot.

3. Add shrimp and heat 4 minutes or until shrimp are warm.

4. Add spaghetti sauce and heat until warm; serve mixture
   over linguine.

Sprinkle with Parmesan cheese, optional.

Soycutash n' Shrimp Gluten Free

1 package (frozen) TJ's Soycutash

2 tablespoons water

1 stalk celery, chopped

1/4 cup chopped red onion

1 teaspoon TJ's Crushed Garlic,
   or 3 garlic cloves, minced

1 to 2 jalapeño peppers, split lengthwise
   and cut crosswise into thin strips

3 tablespoons white wine

1 pound (frozen) TJ's medium shrimp, uncooked or cooked

1/4 teaspoon freshly ground black pepper

2 tablespoons chopped fresh parsley

3 tablespoons soy bacon bits, optional

Serves 4

Per serving:
234 calories
4.2 g fat
282 mg sodium
21 g carbohydrate
5 g fiber
26 g protein

1. Prepare Soycutash according to package directions; drain.

2. In a skillet over medium-high heat, add 2 tablespoons
   water; add celery, onion, garlic, jalapeño and wine; cook
   2 minutes, stir often.

3. Stir in Soycutash and cook 4 minutes, stir often.

4. Add shrimp; cook 5 minutes or until shrimp are cooked
   (or warm in the case of cooked shrimp), stir often.
   Remove from heat.

5. Stir in pepper; sprinkle with parsley and bacon, if desired.

Serve immediately.

Shrimp Pizza

1 bag (refrigerated) TJ's Wheat
   Pizza Dough

1 cup TJ's Low Fat Tuscano Marinara
   Sauce (can)

8 ounces (frozen) TJ's Medium Cooked
   Shrimp, thawed and rinsed

2 cups sliced well-rinsed leeks
   (white and green parts)

1/4 teaspoon red pepper flakes

Freshly ground black pepper to taste

1/4 cup freshly grated Parmesan cheese

Serves 4

Per serving:
391 calories
5.8 g fat
884 mg sodium
58 g carbohydrate
8 g fiber
21 g protein

Options:
Use prepared pizza crust.

Use your favorite marinara or spaghetti sauce.

1. Place the oven rack on the lowest rung and preheat the oven to 450°F.

2. Form the pizza dough into a circle and place it on a pizza pan sprayed with vegetable oil or olive oil.

3. Spray the surface of the dough with oil and place on the bottom rack of the oven; cook 10 minutes.

4. Slice shrimp in half lengthwise.

5. In a large saucepan, heat water and cook the leeks, stir often for 5 minutes or until they are tender; drain.

6. Spread the tomato sauce evenly over the partially-baked crust to within 1/2 inch of the edge.

7. Sprinkle the leeks over the sauce and arrange the shrimp in concentric circles on top of the leeks.

8. Sprinkle Parmesan over the pizza and place pizza on the top shelf of the oven. Bake for 10 to 15 minutes or until crust is brown.

Vegetarian

Mexican

Tofu Tacos Gluten Free

8 TJ's Corn Tortillas or Brown Rice Tortillas

8 ounces TJ's Organic Firm Tofu, cut into small squares

½ (12-ounce) container fresh salsa, or use bottled salsa

1 medium tomato, chopped

¼ cup red onion, sliced, optional

Shredded lettuce

Chopped cilantro

Lime wedges, optional

Grated low-fat cheese, optional

Nonfat sour cream or yogurt, optional

Avocado slices, optional

Serves 4

Per serving:
325 calories
2.75 g fat
170 mg sodium
9.75 g carbohydrate
1.7 g fiber
10 g protein

Options:
Use 2 tablespoons of TJ's Cilantro Salad Dressing in place of fresh salsa and use shredded cabbage in place of lettuce.

Add TJ's Smoky Black Bean Dip to taco filling or use in place of tofu.

Use TJ's Steamed Lentils, TJ's Refried Black Beans, TJ's Cuban Black Beans or TJ's Beef-Less Strips in place of tofu.

Use cooked chicken, TJ's Spicy Jalapeno Chicken Sausage, or cooked shrimp in place of tofu for a non-vegetarian version.

1. Heat tortillas in microwave for 30 seconds each or in oven on a baking tray at 350°F for 5 minutes.

2. Put tofu on a microwavable plate and heat in microwave 50 seconds.

3. Place tofu and other ingredients on tortilla.

Serve as tacos or flat as tostadas, with toppings heaped on top of tofu mixture, if desired.

Serve with nonfat or low-fat refried beans and brown or white rice.

Black Bean and Rice Soup Gluten Free

2 (14.5 ounce) cans TJ's Organic Black Bean Soup

¾ teaspoon ground cumin, or to taste

2 to 5 drops hot sauce, or to taste

1 cup (refrigerated) TJ's Pico de Gallo Salsa, or to taste

1 pouch (frozen) TJ's Brown Rice (organic or regular), or 2 cups cooked rice

2 teaspoons fresh lime juice, optional

Chopped fresh cilantro, optional

Serves 4

Per serving:
187 calories
1.6 g fat
520 mg sodium
40 g carbohydrate
5 g fiber
6.5 g protein

Options:
Add diced chopped organic tofu to add protein while soup is heating.

Add ½ cup diced zucchini while soup is heating.

Use any kind of tomato salsa to replace TJ's Pico de Gallo Salsa.

Garnish with chopped green onions, crumbled feta cheese or TJ's Fancy Shredded Light Mexican Blend cheese.

Add rice to thicken mixture, if needed, and use to fill taco shells or use as burrito filling.

1. Place soup and cumin in saucepan and simmer over medium heat for 5 minutes.

2. Add hot sauce, salsa and rice. Heat ingredients together another 5 minutes, stir occasionally. Add water or vegetable broth to thin if needed.

3. Divide soup into 4 bowls and top with lime juice and cilantro, optional.

Serve with reduced fat tortilla chips and salsa, or serve with gluten-free cornbread.

Lentil Salsa Stew Gluten Free

2 tablespoons water

1 onion, chopped,
   or 1 cup TJ's Diced Onions

1 package TJ's Steamed Lentils

1 pouch (frozen) TJ's Brown Rice
   (organic or regular),
   or 2 cups cooked rice

2 medium carrots, shredded or TJ's
   shredded fresh carrots

2 cups TJ's Organic Hearty Vegetable
   Broth

1 (12-ounce) container TJ's fresh salsa

Chopped cilantro, optional

Nonfat sour cream or yogurt, optional

Serves 4

Per serving:
269 calories
1 g fat
766 mg sodium
54 g carbohydrate
12 g fiber
13 g protein

Option:
Use TJ's Low Sodium
Vegetable Broth.

1. Heat water in a skillet over medium-high heat. Add onions and cook until translucent, about 3 minutes, stir often.

2. Add the rest of the ingredients; turn heat to low and simmer 15 minutes.

3. Ladle stew into 4 bowls; sprinkle with cilantro, optional, and add a dollop of sour cream, optional, and serve.

Gordito

2 tablespoons water

1 onion, chopped,
or 1 cup TJ's Diced Onions

1 each red and green bell peppers,
sliced, or use TJ's Mélange-à-Trios
(frozen bell pepper mixture)

2/3 teaspoon TJ's Crushed Garlic,
or 2 cloves garlic, minced

1/2 teaspoon chili powder

1 cup TJ's sliced fresh mushrooms

1 (32-ounce) can TJ's Unsalted Whole
and Peeled Plum Tomatoes
(use slotted spoon to collect
1 1/2 cups tomatoes)

1 (12-ounce) package TJ's Beef-Less
Ground Beef

1/4 teaspoon coarse ground black
pepper

Chopped cilantro, optional

4 TJ's Flatbreads

Serves 4

Per serving:
288 calories
7 g fat
696 mg sodium
43 g carbohydrate
6.2 g fiber
21 g protein

Options:
Use Smart Ground Mexican Style in place of "Original" and omit chili powder.

Use whole wheat or other tortillas in place of flatbread.

Top flatbreads with TJ's Fancy Lite Mexican Blend cheese.

Add chopped lettuce, chopped tomatoes, or sliced avocado.

Add a teaspoon or two of lime juice after adding beef.

Top Gordito with nonfat sour cream or yogurt or TJ's Creamy Cilantro Dressing.

1. In a large skillet, heat water on medium-high heat; add onions, peppers and garlic; cook for 3 minutes, stir occasionally.

2. Add chili powder and mushrooms; continue cooking for 5 minutes.

3. Add marinara sauce; bring to a boil and reduce heat to low and simmer, uncovered, 15 minutes. Add chopped cilantro.

4. Add Beef-less Ground Beef and pepper; cook 2 minutes, stir occasionally.

Top flatbread with gordito mixture, fold and serve.

Portobello Mushroom Fajitas

2 tablespoons water

⅓ teaspoon TJ's Crushed Garlic,
  or 1 clove garlic, minced

1 teaspoon ground cumin

½ teaspoon chili powder

¾ pound fresh portobello or crimini
  mushrooms, thinly sliced

2 cups (frozen) TJ's Mélange-à-Trois
  (frozen bell pepper mixture)

½ onion, chopped,
  or ½ cup TJ's Diced Onions

8 ounces TJ's Organic Firm Tofu,
  chopped

2 tablespoons lime juice

¼ cup chopped fresh cilantro

6 TJ's Whole Grain Flour Tortillas

TJ's fresh salsa

½ cup low fat sour cream or yogurt,
  optional

Serves 6

Per serving:
190 calories
4.3 g fat
388 mg sodium
31 g carbohydrate
3.6 g fiber
7 g protein

Options:
Use TJ's Creamy Cilantro
Salad Dressing mixed
with a little bit of
mayonnaise in place of
sour cream or yogurt.

Use TJ's Beef-less strips
in place of tofu.

Use TJ's Brown Rice
Tortillas to make recipe
gluten free.

1. Heat water in a large skillet over medium-high heat; add
   garlic, cumin, chili powder, mushrooms, bell peppers
   and onion. Reduce heat to medium and cook mixture 4
   to 6 minutes, stir often, until vegetables are tender. Add
   chopped tofu, stir and heat 3 minutes.

2. Sprinkle lime juice and cilantro over vegetable-tofu mixture.

3. Heat tortillas in microwave (30 seconds each).
   For alternative heating instructions see page 30.

4. Spoon ½ cup vegetable mixture onto each tortilla; roll up.

Top with salsa and sour cream, if desired.

Serve with rice and beans.

Vegetarian

Asian and Indian

Apricot Lentil Soup Gluten Free

2 tablespoons water

¾ onion, chopped,
    or ¾ cup TJ's Diced Onions

½ teaspoon TJ's Crushed Garlic
    or 1½ cloves garlic, minced

3 Roma (plum) tomatoes, peeled
    and chopped

¾ teaspoon ground cumin

½ teaspoon dried thyme

¼ cup dried apricots, chopped (about 10 halves)

1 package (refrigerated) TJ's Steamed Lentils

2 cups TJ's Organic Hearty Vegetable Broth

1½ tablespoons fresh lemon juice

Freshly ground black pepper, to taste

Serves 4

Per serving:
191 calories
0.3 g fat
573 mg sodium
15 g carbohydrate
11 g fiber
13 g protein

1. Heat 2 tablespoons water to medium-high heat in a large soup pot.
2. Add onions and garlic and cook about 3 minutes.
3. Add tomatoes and spices (with the exception of lemon juice); continue to cook for another 2 to 3 minutes.
4. Add apricots, lentils and broth; simmer for 5 minutes.
5. Add lemon juice and pepper to taste.
6. Purée half of soup mixture then return to pot.

Serve warm.

Easy Curry Vegetables and Tofu GlutenFree

1 package (frozen) TJ's Stir Fry
  Vegetables

1/2 cup TJ's Curry Simmer Sauce

1/4 cup TJ's Light Coconut Milk

6 ounces TJ's Organic Firm Tofu,
  cubed

Place ingredients in a small saucepan
over medium heat and stir occasionally
for 6 to 7 minutes, or put in microwave-
safe dish and microwave for 3 minutes.

Serve over rice or quinoa.

Serves 2

Per serving:
255 calories
9.7 g fat
457 mg sodium
25 g carbohydrate
7.5 g fiber
17 g protein

Options:
Use (refrigerated) cut-
up vegetables such
as Asian Stir Fry or
Asparagus Sauté.

Use baked tofu.

Add vegetable broth
and make soup.

Spinach Mushroom Curry Gluten Free

2 tablespoons water

½ onion, chopped,
  or ½ cup TJ's Diced Onions

⅓ teaspoon TJ's Crushed Garlic,
  or 1 clove garlic, minced

3 small potatoes, chopped

1 package TJ's Crimini mushrooms,
  sliced

1 can TJ's Garbanzo beans, rinsed

½ cup TJ's Curry Simmer Sauce

½ cup TJ's Light Coconut Milk
  (or use ¼ cup regular coconut
  milk and ¼ cup water)

2 (6-ounce) bags TJ's Organic Baby
  Spinach, or use frozen spinach

⅛ teaspoon curry paste,
  or more to taste, optional

1 teaspoon curry powder,
  or Garam Masala, optional

¼ cup chopped cilantro, optional

Serves 4

Per serving:
290 calories
5 g fat
535 mg sodium
51 g carbohydrate
12 g fiber
13 g protein

Options:
Use TJ's Masala Simmer
Sauce, Yellow Thai Curry
Simmer Sauce or Thai
Red Curry Simmer Sauce
in place of Curry Simmer
Sauce.

Use parsnips or cauliflower
in place of potatoes.

Use lentils or tofu in place
of garbanzo beans.

Use kale in place of spinach, or use half spinach
and half kale.

1. Heat large skillet over medium heat; add water and
   cook the onions and garlic for about 2 minutes.

2. Add potatoes and stir often for 4 minutes or until fork-
   tender when pierced.

3. Add mushrooms, bean and sauces. Stir while heating
   for about 2 more minutes.

4. Stir in spinach and cook for another 3 minutes until
   wilted. Add optional spices and cilantro.

Serve with TJ's Brown Rice.

Peanut Pasta with Tofu

Marinade:

1/4 cup TJ's Rice Vinegar

2 teaspoons TJ's Toasted Sesame Oil

2 tablespoons TJ's Reduced Sodium
  Vegetable Broth

1 tablespoon TJ's Reduced Sodium
  Soy Sauce

1 teaspoon sugar

1 package TJ's Organic Firm Tofu cut
  into 1/2-inch cubes (gently squeeze
  out excess water before cubing)

8 ounces TJ's Penne Pasta

3 cups (frozen) TJ's Stir Fry Vegetables

Sauce:

2/3 teaspoon TJ's Crushed Garlic, or 2 cloves garlic, minced

1/4 cup TJ's Crunchy Peanut Butter, natural style

1/8 teaspoon ground ginger

4 tablespoons water

1/4 cup sliced green onions

1/3 cup chopped cilantro leaves, optional

Cilantro sprigs as garnish

Crushed red pepper flakes, optional

Serves 6

Per serving:
302 calories
10 g fat
542 mg sodium
31 g carbohydrate
3.6 g fiber
18 g protein

Options:
Add 1/2 cup plum
jam after adding
tofu.

Use 1/2 cup TJ's
Asian Style Spicy
Peanut Vinaigrette
in place of mari-
nade.

1. For marinade: in a medium bowl mix vinegar, 1 teaspoon of the oil, broth, soy sauce and sugar; add tofu; set aside and stir occasionally.

2. Cook pasta according to package directions. While water heats, gather ingredients for sauce.

3. When pasta is al dente or tender to the bite add stir-fry vegetables and cook for 2 more minutes; drain.

4. Remove tofu from marinade and reserve the extra for use in the sauce.

5. In a large skillet, heat remaining 1 teaspoon oil; toss in garlic and stir, cooking just until fragrant, about 30 seconds.

6. Add peanut butter, excess marinade from tofu and ginger; cook just until sauce is smooth and well blended.

7. Add 4 tablespoons water and continue to stir.

8. Remove from heat and add pasta mixture, green onions and cilantro leaves, if desired; mix gently but thoroughly.

9. Mix in tofu and garnish with cilantro sprigs.

Season to taste with red pepper flakes, optional.

Asian Stir Fry Vegetables with Tofu and Peanut Vinaigrette

2 tablespoons water

2/3 teaspoon TJ's Crushed Garlic,
   or 2 cloves garlic, minced

1 package (frozen) TJ's Stir Fry Vegetables

1/2 package (7 ounces) TJ's Organic
   Firm Tofu, cubed

1 pouch (frozen) TJ's Brown Rice
   (organic or regular),
   or 2 cups cooked rice

1/3 cup (refrigerated) TJ's Asian Style Spicy
   Peanut Vinaigrette

3 tablespoons TJ's Satay Peanut Sauce,
   or more to taste

1/8 teaspoon chili paste, optional

1/4 cup chopped cilantro, optional

2 tablespoons chopped peanuts, optional

Pinch of red pepper flakes, optional

Serves 4

Per serving:
295 calories
8.8 g fat
249 mg sodium
42 g carbohydrate
5.25 g fiber
14 g protein

Options:
Use edamame
in place of tofu.

Add TJ's Just
Chicken or cooked
grilled strips or
shrimp to make
a non-vegetarian
version.

1. Heat large skillet over medium heat; add water and cook garlic for about 2 minutes.

2. Add tofu and vegetables and stir often for 4 to 6 minutes or until vegetables are fork-tender when pierced.

3. Add tofu and rice and stir for 2 minutes.

4. Add vinaigrette and peanut sauce and stir until warm, about 2 minutes.

Add optional items to taste.

Asian Style Brown Rice Tofu Salad

2 pouches (frozen) TJ's Brown Rice
(organic or regular),
or 4 cups cooked rice

½ cup peas, thawed if frozen

3 green onions, chopped

½ cup chopped celery

½ teaspoon bottled crushed or minced
ginger, or freshly grated ginger

¼ cup chopped cilantro

2 tablespoons chopped peanuts

3 tablespoons (refrigerated) TJ's Asian
Style Spicy Peanut Vinaigrette

1 teaspoon TJ's Rice Vinegar

Pinch of red pepper flakes, optional

4 ounces (refrigerated) TJ's baked flavored tofu, cubed

Serves 4

Per serving:
337 calories
7.5 g fat
284 mg sodium
50 g carbohydrate
6.8 g fiber
10 g protein

Option:
Use TJ's Satay Peanut
Sauce in place of
vinaigrette.

1. Heat rice according to package directions, let cool if desired.
2. Combine all of the ingredients in a large bowl and stir
   together gently.

Serve warm or cold.

Asian Style Pumpkin Soup Gluten Free

2 tablespoons water

²⁄₃ cup chopped green onions

½ cup chopped celery

½ cup (refrigerated) TJ's snow peas, sliced into ½-inch pieces

²⁄₃ teaspoon TJ's Crushed Garlic, or 2 cloves garlic, minced

1 teaspoon bottled crushed or minced ginger, or freshly grated ginger

2 cups TJ's Organic Pumpkin, or other canned pumpkin

2 cups TJ's Organic Hearty Vegetable Broth

1 (14-ounce) can TJ's Light Coconut Milk

1 teaspoon red curry paste, to taste

1 tablespoon lime juice

4 tablespoons chopped cilantro

Serves 4

Per serving:
118 calories
6.8 g fat
334 mg sodium
12 g carbohydrate
5.7 g fiber
3.4 g protein

Options:
Add cubed tofu the last 5 minutes.

Use bok choy in place of celery.

Use 1 cup (frozen) TJ's Stir Fry Vegetables in place of celery and snow peas.

Use TJ's Cut Sugar Pumpkin, or cubed kabocha squash (both are seasonal), in place of the canned pumpkin. Allow longer cooking time.

1. In a large saucepan, heat water over medium heat. Add the onions and celery, cook for 7 to 10 minutes.

2. Add the snow peas, garlic and ginger and cook 2 minutes more.

3. Stir in the pumpkin and broth; cook for another 5 minutes and stir often.

4. Stir in the coconut milk, curry paste and lime juice, stir until heated through.

Serve soup in bowls and garnish with the cilantro.

Curry Tofu with Couscous

1 cup water

½ cup TJ's dried couscous

2 tablespoons TJ's Curry Simmer Sauce, or Masala Simmer Sauce

3 ounces TJ's Organic Firm Tofu, cubed

¼ cup (frozen) TJ's peas

1 tablespoon chopped cilantro

10 chopped peanuts, optional

Serves 2

Per serving:
273 calories
5.8 g fat
220 mg sodium
42 g carbohydrate
4.75 g fiber
6 g protein

Options:
Use whole wheat couscous to increase fiber.

Add potatoes and add more Curry Simmer Sauce.

Add sweet potatoes, parsnips, spinach and light coconut milk for variety.

1. Heat 1 cup water to nearly boiling and add ½ cup couscous. Cover and let stand 5 minutes. Fluff with a fork.

2. Combine Curry Simmer Sauce, tofu and peas; heat in microwave for 2½ minutes, or in medium-size saucepan on the stove for 4 minutes.

3. Place tofu over couscous and add cilantro and chopped peanuts.

Quick Carrot Ginger Coconut Soup

4 cups TJ's Carrot Ginger Soup

2 teaspoons peanut butter

1/2 cup TJ's Light Coconut Milk

1/2 teaspoon TJ's Crushed Garlic,
   or 1 1/2 cloves garlic, minced

1 teaspoon red pepper flakes, to taste

Chopped cilantro, optional

Serves 4

Per serving:
105 calories
4 g fat
426 mg sodium
16 g carbohydrate
1 g fiber
2 g protein

Options:
For a heartier soup, add canned Northern White Beans, TJ's Steamed Lentils or cubed organic tofu.

Add snow peas, water chestnuts or broccoli.

1. Combine all ingredients, with exception of cilantro, in a large microwave-safe bowl or medium-size sauce pan.

2. Heat in microwave for 3 minutes or in a medium-size saucepan on stove top for 7 minutes until warm. Be sure not to boil.

Sprinkle with chopped cilantro, optional.

Quinoa Peanut Tofu Gluten Free

½ cup TJ's Organic Quinoa (white or red)

¼ cup TJ's Satay Peanut Sauce*

4 ounces TJ's Organic Tofu

Chili paste, optional

Chopped cilantro, optional

Serves 2

Per serving:
265 calories
9 g fat
210 mg sodium
36 g carbohydrate
3.1 g fiber
12.5 g protein

Options:
Add ¼ cup light coconut milk.

Add cooked snow peas and water chestnuts.

Add 1 cup finely chopped kale and 2 tablespoons more peanut sauce.

1. Prepare quinoa according to package directions.

2. Add satay sauce and tofu, chop into bite-size cubes; add chili paste and cilantro, if desired.

Serve warm or cold.

*Contains fish sauce.

Tofu Stir Fry with Almonds

2 pouches (frozen) TJ's Brown Rice,
(organic or regular),
or 4 cups cooked rice

Sauce:

3 tablespoons TJ's Reduced Sodium
Soy Sauce

2 tablespoons sake, or dry sherry

1 teaspoon sugar

1 teaspoon peanut oil

1 teaspoon sesame oil

1 ¼ (12-ounce) packages TJ's Broccoli florets, or 1 pound
broccoli, cut into small florets, stalks peeled and cut into
small bite-size pieces

5 ounces (refrigerated) TJ's flavored baked tofu, cubed

⅓ to ⅔ teaspoon TJ's Crushed Garlic,
or 1 to 2 cloves garlic, minced

1 ounce TJ's chopped or slivered almonds

4 to 5 green onions, cut into 1-inch pieces

Black pepper or cayenne pepper to taste

Serves 4

Per serving:
343 calories
9 g fat
658 mg sodium
51 g carbohydrate
7.4 g fiber
14 g protein

1. Heat rice according to package directions; keep warm.

2. Mix soy sauce with sake or sherry and sugar in a small
bowl or cup; set aside.

3. Heat a wok or large saucepan to medium-high heat; add
1 teaspoon peanut oil and 1 teaspoon sesame oil. Stir-
fry broccoli first, then add tofu, then garlic, almonds and
onions; continue to stir another 2 minutes.

4. Add the soy sauce mixture; season with pepper or cayenne
pepper, if desired.

Serve with rice.

Peanut-Tamarind Sweet Potato Curry Gluten Free

1 pouch (frozen) TJ's Brown Rice (organic or regular), or 2 cups cooked rice

2 tablespoons water

1 onion, chopped, or 1 cup TJ's Diced Onions

1 pound sweet potatoes, peeled and cubed into 1-inch squares

2 teaspoons bottled crushed ginger, or 3 teaspoons freshly grated ginger

1 jalapeno chili, seeded and minced

1 teaspoon curry powder

$\frac{1}{2}$ cup TJ's Organic Hearty Vegetable Broth

$\frac{3}{4}$ cup TJ's orange juice

$\frac{1}{4}$ cup TJ's Crunchy Peanut Butter, natural style

1 tablespoon brown sugar

1 teaspoon tamarind paste, or lime juice

$\frac{1}{2}$ teaspoon salt

Serves 4

Per serving:
320 calories
10 g fat
456 mg sodium
52 g carbohydrate
6.8 g fiber
8 g protein

Options:
Use butternut squash in place of sweet potatoes.

To increase protein, add lentils, tempeh, or tofu.

Adapted from "Vegetarian Times."

1. Heat rice according to package directions; keep warm.

2. Heat water in skillet over medium-high heat. Add onions and cook until translucent, about 3 minutes.

3. Add sweet potatoes and cook 1 minute. Add ginger and jalapeño; stir and cook 1 minute. Stir in curry powder and cook 1 minute more.

4. Add broth, cover, and reduce heat to medium-low and simmer 10 minutes or until sweet potatoes are soft.

5. Whisk together juice, peanut butter, sugar, tamarind paste, or lime juice and salt in bowl. Add to sweet potato mixture and bring to a simmer. Cook 5 minutes or until sauce thickens. Serve over rice.

Spinach Salad with Tofu and Asian Vinaigrette

3 cups TJ's packaged fresh spinach, rinsed and dried

2 ounces TJ's Organic Extra Firm Tofu, cubed

2 stalks TJ's Hearts of Palm, sliced, optional

2 tablespoons chopped fresh basil, or more to taste

1 tablespoon TJ's Asian Style Spicy Peanut Vinaigrette

1 tablespoon TJ's Rice Vinegar

1½ tablespoons soy bacon bits or Bacos

Serves 1

Per serving:
203 calories
10 g fat
587 mg sodium
14 g carbohydrate
4 g fiber
8 g protein

Options:
Use Northern White Beans or baked tofu in place of tofu.

Use seasoned rice vinegar in place of rice vinegar – it will add 6 grams of sugar per tablespoon.

1. Assemble salad with first 4 ingredients, toss.

2. Mix vinaigrette and vinegar together and drizzle over salad.

3. Sprinkle bacon bits over salad.

Vegetarian

Everything else

Spaghetti with Tofu

8 ounces spaghetti

2 tablespoons water

1 onion, chopped,
   or 1 cup TJ's Diced Onions

1 teaspoon TJ's Crushed Garlic,
   or 1 clove garlic, minced

1 package TJ's Organic Extra Firm
   Tofu, cubed

1 medium zucchini, sliced

2 cups TJ's Marinara sauce

Parmesan cheese, optional

Serves 4

Per serving:

313 calories
7.4 g fat
512 mg sodium
37 g carbohydrate
6.3 g fiber
23 g protein

Options:
Use whole wheat
spaghetti to increase
fiber.

Add fresh tomatoes,
other kinds of
summer squash,
mushrooms, bell
peppers, etc.

Use TJ's Meatless
Meatballs in place
of tofu.

1. Prepare spaghetti according to package directions; keep warm.

2. Heat water in a skillet over medium-high heat;
   cook onion and garlic until onions are translucent, about
   3 minutes.

3. Add tofu and zucchini and cook 4 minutes more.

4. Heat Marinara sauce in a medium-size saucepan over
   medium-high heat for about 6 minutes or until desired
   temperature. Or microwave in a microwave-safe dish for
   up to 2 minutes to desired temperature.

Serve spaghetti topped with sauce and tofu mixture. Sprinkle
with Parmesan, if desired.

Lentil Ragout [Gluten Free]

3 packages TJ's Cut Butternut Squash,
  or 1½ pounds butternut squash,
  peeled and cut into 1-inch cubes

2 tablespoons water

1 onion, chopped,
  or 1 cup TJ's Diced Onions

⅔ teaspoon TJ's Crushed Garlic,
  or 2 cloves garlic, minced

2 cups (refrigerated) TJ's Steamed Lentils

1 teaspoon ground cumin

½ teaspoon ground cinnamon

1 vegetable bouillon cube, crushed

½ cup dried apricots, cut into quarters, soaked in hot water

1 cup plum tomatoes, diced

2 tablespoons lemon juice

1 tablespoon chopped parsley

Serves 4

Per serving:
223 calories
6 g fat
510 mg sodium
46 g carbohydrate
12 g fiber
11 g protein

1. Prepare butternut squash according to package directions.

2. Heat 2 tablespoons water in skillet and cook onion and garlic until translucent, about 3 minutes.

3. Add cooked lentils, cumin, cinnamon, bouillon cube, apricots, tomatoes, butternut squash and lemon juice.

4. Cook 5 minutes or until mixture is heated throughout.

5. Add chopped parsley, mix and serve.

Penne Peperonata with Beans and Basil

1 package (frozen) TJ's Penne
  Peperonata

1 cup cannellini beans, rinsed and
  drained

½ cup fresh chopped basil

¼ cup grated Parmesan cheese, optional

Serves 4

Per serving:
286 calories
5 g fat
287 mg sodium
49 g carbohydrate
8.3 g fiber
11.8 g protein

Options:
Add tofu in place of beans.

Add TJ's Italian Chicken Sausage or chicken strips for a non-vegetarian version.

Use other TJ's (frozen) Italian pasta dishes in place of the penne.

1. Cook the penne and beans according to the penne package directions omitting oil or butter if heated on the stove top.

2. Stir in the chopped basil.

Top with Parmesan, if desired.

Easy Lentil Feta Wraps

6 (8-inch) TJ's Whole Grain Flour Tortillas, or TJ's Brown Rice Tortillas

2 teaspoons water

²/₃ teaspoon TJ's Crushed Garlic, or 2 cloves garlic, minced

2 shallots, finely chopped

½ pound fresh mushrooms, sliced

¼ cup dry white wine

2 cups (refrigerated) TJ's Steamed Lentils

4 ounces TJ's Fat Free Crumbled Feta Cheese

¼ cup chopped TJ's Kalamata olives

½ cup chopped tomato

Serves 6

Per serving:
269 calories
4.8 g fat
713 mg sodium
40 g carbohydrate
7 g fiber
13 g protein

Options:
Use half of the feta cheese, rinse and drain the lentils or cook the lentils yourself without salt to lower sodium.

1. Preheat oven to 240ºF. Place sheets of wax paper between tortillas and wrap them in aluminum foil; place in the oven and heat about 10 minutes or until soft. Or, heat each one individually in a flat hot skillet until warm and soft when the lentil mixture is ready to serve.

2. Heat water in saucepan over medium heat and cook the garlic, shallots, and mushrooms 5 minutes, until lightly browned. Pour in the wine; add the lentils, and cook 3 minutes, just until heated through.

3. Fill each tortilla with a portion of the lentil mixture and fold, or roll.

Top with feta cheese, olives, and tomatoes.

Black Bean and Quinoa Salad Gluten Free

½ cup TJ's Organic Quinoa
  (white or red)

1 cup white corn

2 chopped scallions

½ cup chopped tomatoes

½ cup chopped celery

½ cup chopped green or red peppers

1 (15-ounce) can TJ's Black Beans,
  drained and rinsed

Serves 4

Per serving:
264 calories
8.5 g fat
425 mg sodium
44 g carbohydrate
6.2 g fiber
11 g protein

Option:
Use chopped red
onions, grated carrots
or other vegetables,
according to season
or preference.

Dressing:

2 tablespoons extra-virgin olive oil

2 tablespoons lemon juice or balsamic vinegar

1 clove garlic, minced

Chopped cilantro or parsley

1. Rinse quinoa. Cook according to package directions. In the
   last five minutes add the corn if using frozen. Drain and cool.

2. Mix the remaining ingredients in a bowl; pour the dressing
   over vegetables; add quinoa and mix well.

3. Add cilantro or parsley.

Best when served cold.

Italian Vegetables with Bruschetta and Beans

Gluten Free

2 tablespoons water

1 onion, chopped,
or 1 cup TJ's Diced Onions

1/3 teaspoon TJ's Crushed Garlic
or 1 clove garlic, minced

2 medium zucchini, sliced

1 fresh medium tomato, chopped

1 red bell pepper, chopped

5 ounces (frozen, thawed) or fresh
spinach

1/2 cup fresh basil, chopped

1/2 cup TJ's Tuscano Marinara Sauce
(can)

1 cup TJ's Northern White Beans,
drained and rinsed

1/2 cup TJ's Bruschetta, fresh or bottled

Fresh grated Parmesan cheese, optional

Serves 4

Per serving:
144 calories
3 g fat
512 mg sodium
25 g carbohydrate
7.6 g fiber
5.6 g protein

Options:
Substitute any marinara or spaghetti sauce for TJ's Tuscano Marinara Sauce

Use organic tofu in place of white beans.

Add eggplant, chard, etc.

1. In a large skillet, heat 2 tablespoons water over medium-high heat. Add onion and garlic and stir for 3 minutes or until onions are translucent.

2. Add the rest of the ingredients through the white beans; lower heat to medium and stir until the vegetables are cooked, about 7 minutes.

3. Add bruschetta and stir lightly. Sprinkle with Parmesan, if desired.

For a gluten-free version, serve over polenta or gluten-free pasta.

Lentil Salad `Gluten Free`

2 cups (refrigerated) TJ's Steamed Lentils

½ cup celery, finely chopped

1 cup steamed green beans, finely cut

¼ cup freshly chopped parsley

¼ cup chopped red onion, optional

Dressing:

1 tablespoon TJ's Organic Yellow Mustard

½ cup TJ's Fat Free Balsamic Vinaigrette

Dash of lemon juice

Salt and pepper to taste, optional

Small head of romaine lettuce, shredded

1 ripe tomato, cut into wedges

¼ cup finely chopped chives

Serves 6

Per serving:
210 calories
4 g fat
702 mg sodium
33 g carbohydrate
6.5 g fiber
6 g protein

Options:
Use canned lentils, rinsed and drained.

Use canned green beans, drained and rinsed.

Substitute lentils with any canned beans, rinsed.

Add chopped red bell pepper to add color and crunch.

1. In a salad bowl, mix cooked lentils, celery, green beans, parsley and onions, optional.
2. Combine dressing ingredients in a small bowl.
3. Toss lentil mixture with dressing.

Serve on shredded lettuce and garnish with tomato wedges and chives.

Butternut Squash White Bean Soup

2 tablespoons water

1 onion, chopped,
    or 1 cup TJ's Diced Onions

⅓ teaspoon TJ's Crushed Garlic,
    or 1 clove garlic, minced

1 teaspoon cinnamon,
    or more to taste

¾ teaspoon cumin, or more to taste

¼ teaspoon cayenne pepper, optional

½ teaspoon chili powder, optional

3 cups TJ's Butternut Squash Soup

1 (14½-ounce) can Mexican-Style
    Stewed Tomatoes, liquid included

1 (15-ounce) can TJ's Cannellini beans,
    or Northern White beans,
    rinsed and drained

⅛ teaspoon ground black pepper

1 vegetarian bouillon cube,
    or equivalent in concentrate

Chopped cilantro, optional

Serves 6

Per serving:
151 calories
1.2 g fat
568 mg sodium
29 g carbohydrate
9.5 g fiber
7 g protein

Options:
Add more beans
or cubed tofu to
increase protein.

Use Sweet Potato
Bisque in place of
Butternut Squash
Soup.

Use stewed tomatoes
and 1 can green chilies
or ½ to 1 teaspoon
hot sauce (to taste) in
place of Mexican-Style
stewed tomatoes.

1. Heat water in medium-size saucepan to medium-high heat.
   Add onions and cook for 3 minutes or until translucent.

2. Add the rest of the ingredients and simmer soup for 10
   minutes.

Top with chopped cilantro, optional.

Greek Pizza

1 bag (refrigerated) TJ's Wheat
Pizza Dough

5 ounces TJ's Roasted Red Peppers,
rinsed and drained

3 ounces TJ's Light Feta cheese,
crumbled

1 (16-ounce) can artichoke hearts,
quartered and rinsed

4 ounces fresh tomatoes, diced

½ onion, chopped,
or ½ cup TJ's Diced Onions

2¼ ounces sliced black olives, rinsed and drained

⅔ teaspoon TJ's Crushed Garlic, or 2 cloves garlic, minced

2 tablespoons fresh basil, chopped or 2 teaspoons dried

2 tablespoons fresh oregano, or 2 teaspoons dried

½ teaspoon freshly ground black pepper

Serves 6

Per serving:
250 calories
5.3 g fat
869 mg sodium
40 g carbohydrate
5.4 g fiber
9.5 g protein

Option:
Use prepared pizza
crust.

1. Place the oven rack on the lowest rung and preheat the oven to 400°F.

2. Form the pizza dough into a circle and place it on a pizza pan sprayed with vegetable oil or olive oil.

3. Spray the surface of the dough with oil and place on the bottom rack of the oven; cook 10 minutes.

4. Spread red peppers over pizza and set aside. Combine the rest of the ingredients and spread evenly over pizza crust.

5. Place pizza on the top shelf of the oven and bake for 10 to 15 minutes, until crust is brown.

Veggie Ranch Pizza

1 bag (refrigerated) Wheat Pizza Dough

½ cup TJ's Low Fat Parmesan Ranch salad dressing

½ cup (2 ounces) TJ's Lite Sharp Celtic Cheddar, shredded

½ cup TJ's Shredded Carrots

½ cup chopped cauliflower

½ cup chopped fresh broccoli

½ onion, chopped, or ½ cup TJ's Diced Onions

½ cup chopped red bell pepper

½ cup sliced fresh mushrooms

¼ cup (1 ounce) TJ's part skim mozzarella cheese, shredded

Serves 4

Per serving:
381 calories
8.5 g fat
797 mg sodium
54 g carbohydrate
7 g fiber
8.5 g protein

Option:
Add TJ's Just Chicken or cooked grilled chicken strips to make a nonvegetarian version.

1. Place the oven rack on the lowest rung and preheat the oven to 450°F.

2. Form the pizza dough into a circle and place it on a pizza pan sprayed with vegetable oil or olive oil.

3. Spray the surface of the dough with oil and place on the bottom rack of the oven; cook 10 minutes.

4. Spread dressing evenly on the partially-baked crust.

5. Sprinkle with Cheddar cheese, followed by vegetables. Top with mozzarella cheese.

6. Place pizza on highest shelf of the oven and bake for 15 to 20 minutes, until vegetables are tender and cheese is melted and lightly browned.

Index

Index

Index

Gluten-free Recipe Index

These recipes, with the specified products, do not contain gluten according to Trader Joe's "No Gluten Ingredients Used" List.

Does not necessarily pertain to optional items listed on recipes or options listed beside recipes.

* Check ingredient list to determine gluten status of honey-mustard dressing.
** Check ingredient list to determine gluten status of fajita or taco mix.
*** Check ingredient list to determine gluten status of bouillon.